Buy the Right Business—At the Right Price
The Guide to Small Business Acquisition

By Brian Knight
and the Associates of
Country Business, Inc.

Buy the Right Business—At the Right Price
The Guide to Small Business Acquisition
By Brian Knight and the Associates of Country Business, Inc.

The material and techniques presented within this book have been specifically designed by personnel connected with Country Business, Inc. and its affiliate organizations. Any persons using this material as their own or representing same are in violation of the U.S. copyright laws and may face legal action.

Published by Upstart Publishing Company, Inc.
    Publishers of Small Business Management Tools
    12 Portland Street, Dover, New Hampshire 03820.
    (800) 235-8866 or (603) 749-5071

Printed in the U.S.A.

Library of Congress Card Catalog Number: 90-71371

ISBN: 0-936894-17-2

AUGUST 1990 FIRST PRINTING

TABLE OF CONTENTS

INTRODUCTION

This manual is an outgrowth of twelve years of assisting thousands of persons and corporations in their efforts to locate and acquire small businesses.

During these years, the associates of Country Business, Inc. (CBI), examined thousands of small businesses of every description in an attempt to find viable companies for acquisition. Country Business was deeply involved in hundreds of successful and unsuccessful attempts to analyze these businesses, make them stronger, finance them, and often prepare business plans for future operations.

From the beginning we addressed ourselves to the question: *What are the specific conditions that must be met for an acquisition to be successful?*

The work which led to the development of this manual was based on field trial and error, as we observed and assisted others in their efforts. Gradually, we pieced together the approach which is reflected in this book and in the operations philosophy of Country Business, Inc.

We learned much, for example, from the regular failure reports of Dun and Bradstreet and from examining as best we could the reasons some business acquisitions made it and others didn't. It was clear that *undercapitalization* was a major cause of failure, and equally clear that careful development of an adequate capitalization plan could avoid this worst of all traps. The section on **Adequate Capitalization** grew out of this work.

We believe strongly in the importance of proper *business planning* and were fortunate enough to find an excellent manual on business planning for small business, *The*

Business Planning Guide, which has since become a best-seller and a classic in its field. In most cases, the actual performance of the business planned with the manual has been consistent with the projections developed by following the book's guidelines, and the businesses themselves have been successful. As a consequence, a **Reasonable and Complete Business Plan** has become another of the conditions we considered essential.

From the start we accepted that proper business decisions should be based on factual information rather than opinion, and as a result we spent a great deal of time and money searching for operating manuals for various types of small businesses, management texts, demographic data useful for market analysis, standard cost data and other information. We discovered that there is a great deal of data out there, information that could transform the most unprepared business owner into a successful entrepreneur if only these information resources were used and followed. Yet it was rare to find a business owner who was making serious use of the basic information resources that were available. **The Effective Use of Information Resources** became another of the conditions in our search for success.

When we first entered the acquisition business, we found that the problem of evaluation was the most serious one to be overcome. In an attempt to see that businesses were properly priced, we called in appraisers, certified public accountants, consultants and others to establish valuation. It was clear that they could not get together on a definition of "earnings" of a small business, much less establish common sense benchmarks for valuation. Often, the valuation of an "expert" for one side would be two or three times the valuation of an "expert" on the other side.

As a result, we reviewed the available literature and developed guidelines and a procedure that could be reproduced in the field for valuing a business. Eventually, this was incorporated into the business data and evaluation forms which appear in this book. The methodology has been reviewed by dozens of informed, experienced accountants and appraisers and tested in hundreds of situations. We feel it now represents an authoritative approach to evaluation that has been proven in the marketplace. If administered by someone who is qualified and trained, it allows the **Proper Acquisition Price and Terms** condition to be met.

As we, ourselves, became more aware of the growing interest in small business at many levels, we discovered that small business had assumed a status in society far greater than it had in earlier decades. When CBI was started, it was still fashionable to think that big business was "where the action was." It is difficult to realize how profoundly this view has changed in the space of a few years! Most of the new jobs in our country are being generated by small business; that almost all of the innovation in our economy is coming from owners of smaller businesses. Business students are rejecting careers in big business in droves and looking closely at small business; and many of the brightest and best of corporate managers, civil servants and others in more institutionalized modes of work are leaving supposedly secure, upwardly mobile careers in search of greater fulfillment and self-actualization through small business ownership.

While the entire book has been to an extent molded by this trend, the last section, **Understanding the Marketplace**, was a direct consequence of these social changes. The new breed of business owner thrills to the concept of a moving, living market environment. Small business ownership is a fluid, dynamic process that requires continual analysis and modification. But how to adjust where the ground rules themselves appear to change continually? We can only attempt to provide a few of our own insights in the hopes that the readers will recognize the need to tune themselves into this essential process.

The other main sections of this book are each based on specific conditions we discovered to be important to a person who decides to face the challenges and rewards of small business ownership.

The combined effect of the eight "conditions" we have established as critical to the success of the acquisition of a small business is significant. Together they represent a far more powerful and effective tool than has been available in the past to a person starting out on an acquisition search. It is almost impossible for us to imagine that anyone who addresses the eight conditions seriously will experience a real failure. They provide a margin of error that should tide the acquirer over most of the serious mishaps or unexpected challenges.

We hope, of course, that this book will be seen as the powerful tool that it is, and not just as an interesting theory or model.

We who are involved in the small business experience owe it to one another to strengthen this kind of process. CBI, through its association with the International Business Brokers Association, has the opportunity to remain current with the latest trends and techniques affecting our industry. To those who use this book, we would be grateful for any information or insight you can give us about how to make it more effective.

Brian Knight
President
Country Business, Inc.
P.O. Box 1071
Manchester Center, VT 05255
(802)362-4710

Chapter One:
Advantages to Small Business Ownership

One of the more interesting discoveries we have made as consultants and agents in small business acquisitions is that the advantages of small business ownership are not widely understood. For example, it comes as a great surprise to some, that Congress has blessed the small business owner with a great deal of tax shelter in various forms.

For those who are constitutionally suited to small business ownership, the freedom and independence involved are even greater rewards than anticipated.

Because so few people understand how important the advantages of small business ownership can be when an acquisition is properly designed, this outline will be a helpful starting point.

I. Those who value their independence will find plenty of it in small business. They will have no one to answer to but themselves. They will be completely responsible for working hours and conditions and for the success or failure of the enterprise.

The small business owner has virtually unlimited freedom of choice to grow or stay small, change businesses, determine the character of a business, determine hours, products, services and organization, etc. Those who are well-suited to small business ownership often consider this the most important reward it offers.

II. The business owner will experience a much broader degree of business and management activities than it is possible to find in most careers. He or she will not be confined to a single management or job activity. This can lead to a far more complete understanding and knowledge of business processes.

III. The rewards will be directly tied to performance. A business owner will not be competing with others in the same organization or be required to work for someone else's goals.

IV.   One can earn an unlimited amount of money if sufficiently capable and committed. Conversely, one can lose everything if not up to the challenges involved.

V.   A small business can offer an unlimited opportunity for creative talents of the owners. Small business ownership can be an ideal existence for people with talent and creative abilities.

VI.   It is possible to make a small business a family operation for those who wish to be closer to their families. Under good circumstances it can be an ideal learning and working environment for young people who are given the opportunity to participate. Conversely, those who do not wish continuous associations in work in addition to home life are well-advised to avoid the pressures a small business can create.

VII.   A small business is probably the best legal tax shelter in existence. Extensive benefits and tax write-offs can be built into a small business operation, particularly when the real estate is owned. Small business owners rarely have to pay substantial taxes until they are earning a substantial amount of money and enjoying an abundant life-style.
        Special benefits can include subsidized living expenses and shelter, transportation, entertainment, company insurance, medical benefits and many others.

VIII.   A small business with real estate assets and responsive management can be virtually inflation-proof.

IX.   A well-run small businesses can be an even better estate-builder than residential or income real estate. With the demand for small business growing and a scarcity of attractive, profitable ones, many owners find themselves with a much greater net worth than they would have had in traditional careers.

X.   A great deal of assistance (far more than most people realize) is available for those wanting to consider small business ownership. A wealth of outstanding information, manuals, industry data, management assistance, courses and helpful organizations make the risk far lower and the rewards far higher than most people believe it will be. (See Step Seven for a detailed bibliography.)

XI.   Small business ownership has an increasing status as the institutional structure of society faces change and challenge. Even small businesses that were once considered routine or unexciting are now commanding great respect as the attractions of small business ownership become more widely recognized.

XII.   It appears that the small business sector of our country is now growing far more rapidly than big business. A major study in 1988 by Prof. David Birch at M.I.T. indicates that small businesses provided virtually all of the net new job formation in our economy in the 1980s. While this trend has peaked, the small business sector is still expected to grow rapidly in the 1990s.

XIII. Those with good basic management training will usually find a major competitive advantage over most competitors. Trained corporate managers often find that their planning, marketing, operating and/or organizational skills give them a major competitive edge. The required skills can be learned and developed by anyone with determination and normal intelligence.

XIV. Many families are able to get a large amount of equity to buy a business as a result of the steep inflation in residential housing in the last twenty years. This equity earns nothing until it is liquidated; by investing it in the earning assets of a small business, a substantial earning power can often be generated.

XV. One is free to choose, within limits, the environment and area that is most pleasing and healthy, entirely according to one's own value system. Those who find their present area of working a problem will have no such restrictions in choosing a small business. Similarly, the small business owner is free to conduct his or her business activities entirely according to personal ethics and values.

Chapter Two:
Questions and Answers About
Small Business Ownership

Q. Isn't small business inherently risky?

A. As a rule, business start-ups have a high degree of risk.

Business acquisitions need not be unusually risky, since the business that has already proved its ability to survive can be analyzed, measured and evaluated with a reasonable degree of accuracy.

The buyer of an existing, going business can reduce risk to a minimum by following this manual. If it is used carefully, the risk will be no greater—and probably less—than the risks involved in working for a large corporation such as downsizing, leveraged buy-outs, and mandatory early retirement.

Q. But can't a small business be wiped out by circumstances entirely beyond the owners' control?

A. According to Dun & Bradstreet, which conducts annual studies of business failures, most failures occur within five years of a business start-up and virtually all failures occur as a result of management shortcomings (including undercapitalization). The failure rate of established small businesses averages about one in four hundred annually.

Risk exists in all walks of life. Many people who have confidence in their own abilities feel that they are most secure when they have the control over their own careers that only business ownership can bring.

Q. Don't you have to work terribly hard as a small business owner?

A.   Yes, and no one who is afraid of doing so should consider small business ownership. Most people find themselves working longer hours than they did as employees.

On the other hand, most successful owners love their work and are so completely fulfilled by the small business experience that they usually don't even consider their long hours and personal sacrifices to be unpleasant.

Q.   Can't small business ownership create a serious strain on family relationships?

A.   It can, and it often will among those whose family ties were weak to begin with. On the other hand, those who have close, supportive family relationships often find them becoming even stronger as a result of the greater amount of sharing of experiences that takes place.

This is a matter for each family to consider and discuss at length. Good understandings are necessary and usually rewarding in families who own small businesses.

Q.   How much money is needed to buy a small business?

A.   Since every small business is unique, it is difficult to generalize. Every situation obviously has to be examined on its own merits.

As a rule, those with less than $50,000 available either from savings, family, or liquidation of residences or investment assets will find it difficult to acquire a business that can reasonably be expected to support a family with funds left over for emergencies, contingencies, working capital, etc. Total available funds of $100,000 or more often will be required.

However, there are exceptions. Those with great determination, a deep commitment, a cooperative family to help in the work and competence in the field chosen can often find an advantageous acquisition and make up in hard work and ability what is lacking in funds.

Q.   How much can one earn in small business?

A.   It depends entirely on the field chosen, the level of investment, the track record of the business, the ability, experience and commitment of the buyers and the quality of business planning and execution that accompany the purchase.

Much of this can be dealt with by establishing intelligent, appropriate criteria as part of a game plan when the search for a small business begins.

Establish your own earnings criteria and stick to them. These earnings may be represented partly in the "fringe benefits" that many small businesses offer, such as subsidized living expenses and tax shelters.

Much of the earnings for several years should be tax sheltered when substantial depreciable assets are included in the purchase.

Given reasonably diligent and competent management, and a sound business and business plan, it should be possible to increase these earnings by 10% (or more) per year over the rate of inflation.

Q. But isn't it true that many people never "make it" or lose everything?

A. Of course. Many businesses that are for sale never should have been started in the first place. Many will limp along year-after-year in a state of bare survival, gradually wearing down their discouraged owners.

These tragic situations can nearly always be avoided by careful analysis, careful business planning and following the advice of competent professionals.

Q. Don't most businesses grow faster during the first few years? How can I make my investment pay off?

A. A 1988 study by Prof. David Birch of MIT showed that most businesses which grow significantly do so after being in existence for ten or more years. Part of the attraction of acquiring a going business is the chance to accelerate its growth and benefit from the consequent increase in value.

Our experience shows that most businesses that have been under the same management for more than three years can be managed more effectively, both by trimming expenses and by seeking new markets or penetrating current markets more deeply. Your business plan will help determine the potential rate of growth for an acquisition.

Q. What professional assistance is needed?

A. An excellent accountant is absolutely essential, as is a good "can-do" attorney who knows how to make things happen.

A good business broker can be very helpful if you are able to locate one who is experienced, honest and well-informed about the business you are considering.

Good commercial bankers are worth their weight in gold. The owner can get great assistance and counsel from such bankers if they are kept completely informed at all times.

Q. How long does it take to locate a satisfactory business and begin operations?

A. Usually, a minimum of three months and often a year or longer, depending on circumstances.

A business acquisition is infinitely more complicated than the purchase of a house or investment real estate. It takes time. There are many traps.

Q. What are some of these traps?

A. Here are a few that we often see, with a few words of advice on each:

    1. The owner will not disclose figures or will hold back key information. *Solution:* Tell him to look for another buyer and leave.

    2. The owner says that much income is "skimmed" or not reported for tax purposes. *Solution:* Treat it as if the hidden earnings do not exist. They probably don't.

    3. You find just the business you want but you are being rushed because there are other interested buyers. *Solution:* Don't be rushed, but don't analyze the deal to death. Some people tend to use excessive analysis as a shield against decision-making. Properly-priced small businesses are usually sold quickly.

    4. You are ready to make the move, but your family and friends say you are crazy to leave the security of your job for such a risky

proposition. *Solution:* You, not your friends or family, are going to live out the rest of your life.

A great many new owners say that friends resisted their decision to the end (possibly because anything that upsets established relationships can be distressing to those who love you).

Many of your friends will ask you—after you have made the move—to find something for them! It happens all the time.

Q.   Is it common to be frightened by such a move?

A.   Everyone who ever moved from the imagined security of a corporate or institutional "nest" to a self-controlled environment will be frightened at times. Your fears will fall into two categories: those that stem from justifiable concerns, and those that represent nervousness about such a complete change of life-style. Don't let the latter immobilize you.

Q.   If you had two pieces of advice to give above all others, what would they be?

A.   Our first advice would be to develop your problem-solving abilities.

We often see people make important decisions emotionally, or in a virtual state of panic, with little or no logical control.

In the process of searching for, buying and then operating a business, countless problems are certain to arise that must be dealt with logically.

There are many excellent problem-solving techniques that can help in dealing with such situations. These techniques are covered in several books on problem-solving available at any library. (See bibliography.)

Rarely will problems become serious if these techniques are applied. In fact, many problems can be converted to opportunities regularly by small business owners who deal with them rationally and calmly.

Our second piece of advice would be to discourage anyone from going into small business who is doing so largely for negative rather than positive reasons.

Small business ownership is not a satisfactory way to deal with personal or business problems; it is a wonderful way to enhance personal and business goals if the goals are deeply felt and if one's abilities and talents are sufficient to the challenge.

For the right people, small business ownership is the best of all possible worlds. But it is completely inappropriate for others. You will probably know if your desire is strong enough. If in doubt, there are some good guidelines in the first section of this manual that will assist you in deciding whether you have the appropriate characteristics for successful small business ownership.

Step One: Matching the Buyer and the Business

CASE IN POINT

The Melsur Corporation of Brattleboro, Vermont, has been leading manufacturer of hard plastic seats, seatbacks, and desk tops for school furniture for over twenty years, with a long, profitable history. Sales were in the $3 million range, with operating profits averaging over 20% of sales when Jason Doubleday and his partner decided to retire.

The sale was subject to some stringent conditions: it had to be a cash sale, with no paper taken back, a fair price, and the buyer had to have a manufacturing background and enough capital to ensure the continued growth and success of Melsur. Hurley Blakeney, the eventual buyer, fit Mr. Doubleday's specifications to a T. He had built Vermont Medical, a Bellows Falls, Vermont, manufacturer of medical equipment, and was searching for a manufacturing company in the $3 to 4 million range. His manufacturing experience and proven interest in maintaining high quality standards were important—and he and Mr. Doubleday hit it off right from the start.

Profitable manufacturing companies in Melsur's size range are in great demand, so Mr. Doubleday could afford to be choosy. Country Business, Inc. showed Melsur to 15 qualified buyers, of whom 13 offered the asking price, in cash. "I had to ask Phil (Phil Steckler, Country Business, Inc. associate) to stop showing it to new buyers when he'd shown it to a dozen or so, "Mr. Doubleday says. "I wanted to find the right buyer, so we weeded the list down to eight, then a final group of four. I figured that Hurley Blakeney was the best of these."

Making the right match between buyer and business is important for all parties involved. The seller wants to make sure that the business continues, and if paper is involved, must be assured that the buyer will be able to run the business successfully. The buyer, on the other hand, must have the qualifications needed to successfully manage the business during the transition to his or her ownership—a frequently difficult period—and beyond.

The most successful owners are those who have chosen businesses that allow them to make full use of their interests, talents and strengths. The forms in this section will help you make the most of those advantages.

No one will have all of the strengths that would be valuable in any given business. But acknowledging weaknesses in various areas allows you to plan ahead and obtain staff or outside help in the required areas.

The forms in this section are designed to help you set clear goals and establish guidelines for what to look for and how to strengthen yourself to meet the challenges of small business ownership.

While there are no "right" or "wrong" answers to any of the questions in the various forms in this section, there are a few basic areas that require special concern. A small business owner should be willing to work long hours and be able to place business interests first when required. It is unlikely that anyone with low independence needs will put up with the demands of small business ownership. An ability to plan ahead is essential.

The form on page 23, Setting Your Criteria, will be helpful in outlining what to look for in selecting a small business. One of the benefits of small business ownership is that it affords such great freedom of choice. Choose an area of the country you enjoy, a type of business that appeals to you, and a size you can handle.

You do not need to submit the completed forms to anyone for review. They are primarily to assist you in thinking through as thoroughly as possible what to look for. The most difficult question to answer is: "What business will be right for me?"

You aren't looking in a vacuum. You already have ideas about what businesses might make sense for you in light of your goals, resources, interests, experience and aptitudes. This first step will help you weed out unsuitable choices and make sure that you make the right match with the business of your choice.

How and where should you start looking for a business to purchase? Your choices are varied. Look for "business for sale" advertisements in newspapers and business journals. Check the listings offered by real estate agents and business brokers. Keep in touch with bankers, lawyers and accountants who might know of available businesses in your areas of interest. Some people have had good results by placing a "business wanted" advertisement in trade journals and similar media.

One of the difficulties in searching for a business is that there are so many offered, sometimes not seriously, and in many cases only advertised once. You can avoid wasting your time following bogus leads, and keep a close scrutiny of businesses for sale by finding a business broker who specializes in working with serious potential buyers and sellers. This will enlarge the scope of your search, help you identify other areas of interest that may elude you at first, and make the information-gathering part of the acquisition process easier. Sellers are no more eager to waste their time with tire-kickers than you are.

Setting Goals

Most of us never get around to writing down our life goals. Set aside time to think this through. Talk with your spouse, family, friends, and others about your goals. The more clearly you can state them, the better your chances of reaching them.

What do you want out of life? You might want to make a certain amount of money, involve your family in the business, be independent, learn to play the violin, help other people. The possibilities are infinite.

Many people find this exercise easier by starting with a list of vague wishes, then asking themselves, "What if I have only ten more years to achieve these goals? Or five years? Or one year? What would I concentrate on?" Don't expect the list to come effortlessly or immediately. Dwell on it. Your goals will change over time, in both substance and detail.

Ten Things You Want From Life

1. _____   6. _____

2. _____   7. _____

3. _____   8. _____

4. _____   9. _____

5. _____   10. _____

This is your starting point. It is not your ending point. Ask yourself: Of the ten things that you want, how many are you getting from your present work? Would small business ownership be more or less likely to help you reach these goals? If you are considering a specific business for acquisition, is it likely to advance the achievement of all of the important goals?

The following form will help you use the power of word association to develop a description of the business you want or, if you are considering a specific business, to develop a format for the further development of the business.

In the "YES" column, put down any words, phrases or statements that fit some aspect of the business environment and service you want to create.

In the "NO" column, put down words that describe what you want to avoid.

Many people will make several pages of such lists and phrases. We suggest that this be done over a period of time. The subconscious mind will often help to make the lists meaningful.

When most of your "YES" and "NO" comments have been entered, select from the "YES" list a description of the business—in *conceptual* terms—that you want to build.

As an example, the founder of CBI, Jim Howard, used this technique to change a real estate company with no sense of mission to the present company by developing the simple slogan, "We sell successful businesses." All of the information programs later developed to help small business owners grew from this initial statement and from other phrases and words on the "YES" list.

The "NO" list can be equally helpful. As you make decisions about what to keep and what to change in a business you own, the "NO" list will serve as a reminder. By eliminating anything on the "NO" side, a strong, consistent image will be projected.

A very successful couple developed the phrase, "Country Things for Country Folks" using this method. The business they developed around this conceptual definition has been written about in dozens of newspapers and magazine articles, described on the "Today Show," and is a continuing source of fulfillment to the owners.

Those who are very literal may have difficulty getting this word association exercise moving. Try it over a period of several days, and let your imagination go. It can be most worthwhile.

As a general guideline, ask yourself—before starting, and before your final listing—what yes or no words or phrases would apply to your business in the following areas. This is by no means an exhaustive list; it is suggested as at most a starting point. (The "YES" and "NO" responses are for example only.)

The Yes-No List

In thinking about the business you would most like to have, apply the following "yes" and "no" words or phrases to describe it. (Use any kind of free association. A few words are used as examples in each to get started. Try to get at least 30–50 words or phrases.)

Business Feature	Yes	No
Quality of business	High Quality Integrity	Shoddy Low Quality
Size	Up to 20 Employees $1-3 million	More than 50 employees more than $10 million
Location	Urban Midwest	Rural East Coast
Type of Business	Manufacturing	Retail
Product	Automotive	High-tech
Customers	Large wholesalers Favor reliability over low price	Small retailers price conscious
Owner Investor	Under $400,000	over $400,000
Growth potential	Moderate	High
Competitive Climate	Moderately competitive	Highly competitive
Employees	Non-family, educated	Low motivation, hostile
Commute?	Less than one hour	No long drives
"Feel" of business	Professional, efficient, taut	Sloppy, relaxed.

Business Feature	Yes	No

Remember the goal of this exercise is to put your subconscious into play. It is not an exercise in linear thinking, but rather a means to help you think discursively, to feel or constructively daydream your way to a business which accurately reflects your personal goals and values. There's little sense in trying to develop a business that will make you miserable—the inevitable consequence of pursuing business goals at odds with your personal values. As you work on this exercise, ask yourself questions such as, "How does it feel? What will I be doing in the business? With whom—customers as well as employees?" The better you can visualize your ideal business, the better your final choice will be.

Small business ownership is a self-selecting profession. Anyone can start or buy a business, whether or not they are experienced, capable or suited to the demands of small business ownership. This raises the failure rate—and makes any intelligent would-be business owner ask whether or not he or she is indeed suited to small business ownership. While we have found no single test or touchstone foolproof, there are strong indicators of probable success.

A number of studies have been made of successful entrepreneurs by such persons as Dr. Jeffrey Timmons of Northeastern University, Dr. David McClelland of Harvard and ourselves as well. This form is based on a synthesis of the available studies, which tend to reveal certain consistent traits.

We should stress that very few successful small business owners will exhibit all of the characteristics suggested. For example, some highly successful owners are hardly "long-distance runners," but rather creative and impulsive types who have learned to control their excesses. We know some pretty successful people who ignore "feedback"— messages from others—yet are brilliant enough and dedicated sufficiently to an idea that they have made real breakthroughs despite their insensitivity to others' opinions.

Nonetheless, most of the traits covered are among those which will contribute to success over a period of time.

Using the traits suggested in completing the form, prepare in writing an outline of your strengths and weaknesses as they relate to small business ownership. Your weaknesses need not be weaknesses at all if you are aware of them and able to compensate for them, either by hiring others to provide offsetting talents or by working to convert a weakness to a strength.

Every person is unique. Almost every business is unique. If you can match your strengths closely with the demands of a particular business, you and the business will be a powerful combination.

SELF-ASSESSMENT QUESTIONS FOR SMALL BUSINESS OWNERSHIP

The following questions are designed to help you assess the probability that you will be comfortable and successful in small business ownership. It is not intended as a scientifically valid test, but rather a reflection of certain characteristics which research has shown to be important in a small business career.

Answer the questions as honestly and objectively as you can. You will grade yourself, and only you stand to "win" or "lose" as a result of any decisions you make about your career.

1. Are you willing to work long hours with few vacations and irregular time off in order to achieve your goals?	☐ YES ☐ NO ☐ UNCERTAIN
2. Are you prepared to place the needs of your business before those of yourself and your family if necessary to preserve the health and continuity of your business?	☐ YES ☐ NO ☐ UNCERTAIN
3. Does your need to be independent and in control of your work environment make it difficult for you to be satisfied working for others?	☐ YES ☐ NO ☐ UNCERTAIN
4. Are you willing to take full responsibility for mistakes you make, without looking for others to blame? Can you learn from these mistakes to improve your performance in the future?	☐ YES ☐ NO ☐ UNCERTAIN
5. Are you able to sustain your energy and motivation in an uncertain or unstable working or economic environment?	☐ YES ☐ NO ☐ UNCERTAIN
6. Are you willing to take a fair amount of risk in the hope of achieving something you want?	☐ YES ☐ NO ☐ UNCERTAIN
7. Do you feel that you have a high degree of self-discipline? Can you apply yourself to a job that needs to be done even when you don't feel like doing it?	☐ YES ☐ NO ☐ UNCERTAIN

8. Are you willing to "be on stage" . . . to know that others are watching, evaluating and counting on you?	☐ YES ☐ NO ☐ UNCERTAIN
9. Do you believe you are able to show "grace under pressure"?	☐ YES ☐ NO ☐ UNCERTAIN
10. Do you have excellent problem-solving abilities, particularly in crises when others are not thinking clearly?	☐ YES ☐ NO ☐ UNCERTAIN
11. Are you willing to go against the mainstream—to persist in a course you believe in even when others disapprove?	☐ YES ☐ NO ☐ UNCERTAIN
12. When things go wrong, do you pick yourself up promptly and move on to another challenge instead of brooding for a long time and feeling a lot of self pity?	☐ YES ☐ NO ☐ UNCERTAIN
13. Do you empathize well with others?	☐ YES ☐ NO ☐ UNCERTAIN
14. Do you have an ability to lead others in a confused or chaotic environment?	☐ YES ☐ NO ☐ UNCERTAIN
15. Are you willing to spend a great deal of time, as long as you are in business, learning about things that are required or will be helpful in the business?	☐ YES ☐ NO ☐ UNCERTAIN
16. Do you enjoy most other people?	☐ YES ☐ NO ☐ UNCERTAIN

17. Do you enjoy working?	☐ YES ☐ NO ☐ UNCERTAIN
18. Do you have (or are you willing to work hard to acquire) a broad range of business management skills?	☐ YES ☐ NO ☐ UNCERTAIN
20. Do you possess a high degree of "information consciousness"? That is, do you usually, before starting off on a new course, go to considerable lengths to gather and use extensive information and data to assist you in planning and decision-making?	☐ YES ☐ NO ☐ UNCERTAIN
21. Do you rely extensively on feedback to test the results of a course of action and make corrections or adjustments as a result?	☐ YES ☐ NO ☐ UNCERTAIN

22. Check the box which most accurately describes how you feel about each statement:	
a. You don't have to "cut ethical corners" to be successful in business.	☐ AGREE ☐ DISAGREE ☐ NOT IMPORTANT
b. People need a "sense of mission" in order to be fulfilled in their work.	☐ AGREE ☐ DISAGREE ☐ NOT VERY IMPORTANT
c. It is very important for business to provide a service that is worthwhile and useful to others.	☐ AGREE ☐ DISAGREE
d. I want the credit for my accomplishments and am willing to take full responsibility for my mistakes.	☐ YES ☐ NO ☐ DON'T CARE MUCH

e. I have a better chance of reaching my goals by working for myself than by working for others.	☐ YES ☐ NO ☐ NO DIFFER-ENCE
f. It is important for a person to have the freedom to be creative in his or her work.	☐ AGREE ☐ DISAGREE ☐ NOT VERY IMPORTANT
g. It is more important to accomplish something worthwhile than to earn a great deal of money.	☐ AGREE ☐ DISAGREE ☐ DON'T KNOW

Scoring the self-assessment questions

Questions   1 - 21   _____ (Number of yes or agree responses)   x 5 =   _____

                          _____ (Number of uncertain responses)   x 5 =   _____

Question   22 a - g _____ (Number of yes or agree responses)   x 5 =   _____

                          _____ (Number of other responses)   x 2 =   _____

                                                               Total   _____

Scores of:

120-140   indicates person likely to thrive in small business.

80 - 120   indicates tendency towards small business ownership with some areas of conflict.

Below 80   indicates person probably not suited for small business ownership.

INTERPRETATION: The "yes" answers define the profile of a person who will have a high chance of success in most small business ventures. The characteristics reflected by the "yes" or "agree" answers indicate an individual with high independence needs, self-control and self-direction, willingness to face a moderate degree of risk and ability to make a high-level of commitment to the success of a venture. Various studies have identified these characteristics in successful small business owners.

No single person is likely to answer all questions "yes" or "agree." Successful owners have as much individuality as any other class of person.

Business management involves a clearly identifiable set of skills. A person who has been successful in one business will usually be successful in another one that is in a completely different field, because the overall skills required are essentially the same.

We have often observed that business owners tend to favor the tasks at which they excel and ignore areas in which they are weak. The most successful owners discipline themselves to spend extra time in areas where they are weak, take courses or study to improve themselves until they can handle the demands of any area of business management.

As a first step, you should give yourself a thorough and ruthlessly honest evaluation with the following form. If it is filled with negative responses, don't be discouraged; help is available. You can find excellent guidance in the library, from small business consultants, from the Small Business Administration's various programs, or at a nearby university with an extension program.

Many couples who have done these exercises find it meaningful for each of them to do the work separately and then to compare the two to discover where nonexistent, complementary, or overlapping skills exist.

SKILLS INVENTORY CHECKLIST

Following is a summary of the principle functions of small business management. A general familiarity with the basics of each function is essential for successful management of most small businesses. Use the functions marked "no" or "uncertain" to map out a study program prior to your acquisition of a business.

I have enough knowledge in this area to operate my own business.

I. SALES AND MARKETING

	YES	NO	UNCERTAIN
A. Market Research			
B. Market Planning			
C. Pricing			
D. Advertising/PR			
E. Sales Management			
F. Customer Service			
G. Personal Selling			
H. Competitive Analysis			
Total			

II. BUSINESS OPERATIONS

A. Purchasing			
B. Inventory Control			
C. Scheduling			
D. Quality Control			
E. Business Growth			
F. Insurance			
Total			

III. FINANCIAL MANAGEMENT

	YES	NO	UNCERTAIN
A. Bookkeeping/Accounting			
B. Budgeting & Deviation Analysis			
C. Cost Control			
D. Credit & Collections			
E. Bank Relations			
F. Break Even Analysis			
G. Cash Flow / Cash Management			
H. Ratio Analysis			
I. Taxes			
Total			

IV. PERSONNEL

A. Interviewing & Hiring			
B. Training			
C. Motivating People			
D. Policies			
E. Communicating			
Total			

V. ADMINISTRATIVE/MANAGEMENT

A. Problem Solving			
B. Decision Making			
C. Leadership			
D. Using Information			
E. Business Law			
F. Methodology/Operations Research			
G. Computers and EDP			
Total			

Total "yes" boxes checked: _____ of 35 possible.

In choosing the kind of business you want, it helps to proceed from a structured consideration of your personal situation and desires to selection criteria for the business. The following form, Setting Your Criteria, has been designed to make this process easier.

You can add direction to your search for the right business by filling out the following form carefully. Keep it with you as you look at businesses. It will help you react more thoughtfully and focus on things that are really important.

SETTING YOUR CRITERIA

I. Geographic area desired

_____ A. Urban
_____ B. Rural
_____ C. Suburban
Region Desired _____

_____
_____
_____

II. Important to be near

_____ A. Good Schools
_____ B. Cultural Environment
_____ C. Big City
_____ D. Relatives or Friends
_____ E. Ocean or Lake
_____ F. Recreation
What Kind? _____

_____

_____ G. Post Exchange (PX)
_____ H. Airport
_____ I. Hospital
_____ J. Comments

III. Desired Income

_____ A. $0 -$10,000
_____ B. $10,000 - $20,000
_____ C. $20,000 - $50,000
_____ D. $50,000 - $75,000
_____ E. Over $75,000

F. Must consider the following
1. _____
2. _____
3. _____

G. Sources and amounts of assured income
1. _____
2. _____
3. _____

H. Required expenditures (e.g. tuition)
1. _____
2. _____
3. _____

I. Savings or investments above business requirements
1. _____
2. _____
3. _____

IV. Desire to pursue the following avocations -

A. _____
B. _____
C. _____
D. _____
E. _____

V. Desire to use these special talents

A. _____

B. _____

C. _____

D. _____

VI. I like to do these things most

A. _____

B. _____

C. _____

D. _____

VII. I dislike these things most

A. _____

B. _____

C. _____

D. _____

VIII. Attitudes about hard work/time off

____ A.   40 Hour or less workweek

____ B.   Retirement business

____ C.   Part-time business

____ D.   Enjoy hard work

____ E.   Work hard now, later taper off

____ F.   Special (explain) _____

Comments _____

_____

IX. Attitude about working together (husband/wife/family)

____ A.   Single wage-earner only

____ B.   Separate careers

____ C.   Work together

D. Special (explain) _____

Comments _____

X. Long-term estate goals

A. Already taken care of

Explain _____

_____

B. Moderately ambitious

Explain _____

_____

C. Not important

Explain _____

_____

D. Ambitious

Explain _____

_____

Comments _____

_____

_____

XI. Goals for children

A. Number of children _____

B. Sexes and ages of children _____

_____

_____

C. Educational goals _____

_____

D. Occupational goals _____

_____

E. Other _____

XII. Most important reasons for wanting a small business

(Amplify these comments as called for in the space below.)

____ A. Environmental considerations

____ B. Better chance of attaining financial goals

____ C. Quit previous employment

____ D. Fired from previous employment

____ E. Dislike city living

____ F. Fed up with corporate life

____ G. Desire for more challenge

____ H. Desire for more independence

____ I. Family can work together

____ J. Desire for creative freedom

____ K. Need a tax shelter

____ L. Desire for individual responsibility

____ M. Need stimulation and variety

____ N. Solve problems in marriage

____ O. Get children out of bad environment

____ P. Desire for increased income

____ Q. Disagreements with current employer

____ R. No future where I am

____ S. Desire to develop unused talents

____ T. Other

Comments _____

_____

_____

_____

_____

_____

_____

XIII. Personal characteristics that will have a bearing on choice

____ A. Conservative

____ B. Liberal

____ C. Sales oriented

____ D. Patient

____ E. Impatient

____ F. Good with numbers

____ G. Not good with numbers

____ H. Hard worker

____ I. Hard player

____ J. Neither

____ K. Outdoor person

____ L. Intellectual

____ M. Social

____ N. Not social

____ O. Need to be in control

____ P. Love working with people

____ Q. Creative

____ R. Good sense of humor

____ S. Not especially good sense of humor

____ T. Worrier

____ U. Long distance runner

____ V. Need for excitement

____ W. Love peace and quiet

____ X. Like action

____ Y. Like business travel

Comments _____

_____

_____

XIV. Major reservations are

____ A. Fear of risk

____ B. Fear of unknown

____ C. Personal shortcomings

____ D. Unexpected reversals

____ E. Impulsive nature

____ F. Giving up present benefits

____ G. Leaving friends

____ H. Potential of getting trapped

____ I. Too much work?

____ J. No recourse if we fail

____ K. Afraid of bad advice

____ L. Afraid of being cheated

Comment _____

XV. Business MUST HAVE these characteristics

A. _____

B. _____

C. _____

D. _____

XVI. Business MUST NOT HAVE these characteristics

A. _____

B. _____

C. _____

D. _____

XVII. In 10 Years, I would like to have achieved these goals

A. _____

B. _____

C. _____

D. _____

XVIII. I would like to deal with these kinds of people

A. _____

B. _____

C. _____

D. _____

XIX. I would not like to deal with these kinds of people

A. _____

B. _____

C. _____

D. _____

XX. I am able to relocate on the following schedule

A. Soonest: _____

B. Latest: _____

XXI. Advisors

A. Attorney: _____

B. Accountant: _____

C. Other Advisor: _____

XXII. Examples of businesses I find unattractive

A. _____

B. _____

C. _____

D. _____

E. _____

XXIII. Examples of businesses I find attractive

A. _____

B. _____

C. _____

D. _____

E. _____

Prepare an accurate statement of your financial condition. You will need it in dealing with various professional people who will assist you. Owners of businesses for sale may legitimately request it before spending time with you. Any reputable broker or intelligent seller will want to make sure that you are financially qualified *before* showing you detailed confidential information on a business.

You don't want to waste time pursuing a business which you can't afford. While many popular books have been written implying the availability of 100% financing, in the real world such deals are seldom encountered. Your financial capability is a key ingredient in the structure of the purchase, and will heavily influence the decisions of bankers and other key players.

Be sure to indicate the present market value of assets such as your residence, valuables, or securities.

If you have excessive short-term liabilities, try to clean them up as soon as possible. You will find it hard to obtain the required financing for a purchase if you don't.

If most of your assets are tied up in forms that are hard to convert to cash, consider putting them on the market before getting deeply involved in a search.

The form that follows is a simplified version of standard personal financial forms used in banks. Ask your banker for several sets of their forms; you may also wish to solicit his or her help in putting your information in the most favorable light.

FINANCIAL STATEMENT

OF _____

AS OF _____ 19 _____

ASSETS   ## LIABILITIES

Cash on hand	$ _____	Notes payable	$_____
Cash in banks			
Checking	_____	Accounts payable	_____
Savings	_____	Life insurance loans	_____
Certificates of Deposit	_____	Mortgages	_____
IRA/KEOGH	_____		_____
U.S. treasury notes	_____		
Notes receivable	_____	Other loans	_____
Accounts receivable	_____		_____
Loans receivable	_____		_____
Life insurance - cash	_____	Taxes owed	_____
Surrender value	_____	Other liabilities	_____
Marketable securities	_____		_____
Other securities	_____		_____
Vehicles,			
Fair market value	_____	TOTAL LIABILITIES $_____	
Real estate,			
Fair market value	_____		
Other assets	_____		
	_____		
	_____		
TOTAL ASSETS	$_____	NET WORTH	$_____

Summary

Choosing the right business is most readily achieved by consulting your goals and interests, strengths, weaknesses and financial capability. Running a small business successfully requires staunch efforts and considerable perseverance. Without a good fit between you and your business, such steadfastness is questionable. You can acquire business and management skills. You can hire talents to fill weak areas, and leverage your assets to provide proper financing (sometimes bringing on other investors).

But there is no substitute for a tight fit between your goals and interests and the demands of the business.

When you list your goals, you bring your personal goals up for scrutiny. The "Yes-No" List makes a qualitative, conceptual description of the right business (right equals right for you) possible. The Self-Assessment Questions tighten your focus on your aptitude for small business ownership. The Skills Inventory Checklist helps you identify your own strengths and weaknesses, while the Setting Your Criteria section provides a good tool for screening out unsuitable businesses. The Personal Financial Statement acts as a gate: either you are financially qualified or you are not. If not, you have options, ranging from putting your dream off for a few years until you do qualify, or involving other investors.

Step Two: A Thorough Analysis of a Business' Strengths and Weaknesses

CASE IN POINT

Since most transactions involve seller financing, you have to know the company's strengths and weaknesses. You will apply for the business out of cash flow, and any advance knowledge of how to ensure that cash flow will be welcome.

When Ed McCue's home health care company, Aid and Assistance of Southern Maine, went on the market, a management audit showed that it had three very strong points: it was certified by the state, had Medicare certification, and a ideal location for expansion. On the shortcomings side, the company was undercapitalized and lacked the management skills necessary for expanding the business.

Don Giancola, the Country Business, Inc. associate working with Mr. McCue, says that, "When I looked at the business to see who a likely buyer might be, I realized that there would have to be a synergy between Aid and Assistance and the buyer, so that Aid and Assistance would be a natural acquisition. The buyer would need a broad base in the health care industry to bolster credibility with the state licensing people and with doctors. He or she would also need financial stability and the necessary management expertise."

Always look at five general areas: Finances, Marketing, Personnel, Assets, and Risks. Underlying our analysis is the conviction, based on long experience, that a well-run, owner-managed business adequately covers all management aspects. If we find, for example, that a manufacturing business has excellent technical and financial strengths, we want the new and present powers to build on those assets. If the audit shows some marketing weaknesses, then we recommend ways that the new owner can fill in the gaps.

This section contains a very complete Business Data Form which will assist you in gathering all essential information. It also has a Business Inventory Form that will allow you to review, function by function, every aspect of a business you are considering to determine its strengths and weaknesses. Good management is, stated simply, building on the strengths and taking corrective measures to lessen the effect of weaknesses.

The Business Data Form (BDF) should be completed in all necessary detail *before* you start to develop your evaluation. Your ability to obtain accurate data and the willingness of the seller to provide it should influence your decision to proceed. Don't take shortcuts—the valuation process is complicated and you must take the necessary time to do a thorough job. If you aren't willing to take pains at this stage, you should question your suitability for small business ownership.

The business analysis that results from the BDF can be compared to the personal inventory you took in Step One. It may be useful in spotting areas of special concern. For example, if the business records are in poor shape, and you are weak at financial controls and reporting, you would be well-advised to line up professional accounting help in advance of acquiring a business to assist you in setting up effective, useful records. If the business is weak in sales and marketing, and you are weak in these areas, you may need a second-in-command who is strong in these areas.

The analysis of strengths and weaknesses will be addressed in detail in the Business Plan, covered in Step Four.

Just as you went through a process of analyzing your own strengths and weaknesses, you must make a careful analysis of the strengths and weaknesses of a business you are considering buying.

Public accounting firms and manufacturers provide detailed analysis of certain industries. For instance the accounting firm Lau & Wer have provided detailed analysis of the restaurant industry for years; Eli Lilly, a pharmaceutical manufacturer, provides an analysis of drugstore operating trends for a modest fee.

Find out what publications are read by the owners of your business area interest and obtain back copies. They will often contain data sources and operating trends.

Many sellers will be candid about the faults of their business. But you must assume that there are hidden weaknesses, perhaps misunderstood by the owner himself, that must be understood correctly if you are to be successful.

As a first step, gather the type of information suggested in the list on page 37. Do not do business with an owner who will not give you whatever data you need to make an informed judgment. Use the Business Data Form to aid you in gathering the required information.

Second, use the Business Inventory Form to help you address each facet of the business.

Third, pay a visit to your local library and ask the librarian to help you find pertinent books and other information about the type of business you are interested in. At the very least, consult the *Small Business Sourcebook*, published in three volumes by Gale Research, Inc., and make note of the information for your line of business it contains. Since it covers over 200 different lines of business, the odds are you will find a rich source of directly applicable information. If your library doesn't have this *Sourcebook*, find a library that does: it contains references to valuable information sources ranging from books to government programs to seminars, trade associations, and trade financial ratios and will save you hundreds of hours of research.

The "standard cost data" compiled by Robert Morris Associates in their annual *Statement Studies* is important. Your banker has a copy of the most recent figures available; he or she will help you apply this information to the business you are investigating.

If possible, obtain an operations manual such as those prepared by the Bank of America in their *Small Business Reporter* series if one is available for the type of business you are investigating. Your trade association's education department (most have one) is a good source for this kind of very specific information.

A qualified business broker will have all of this information available and will be willing to discuss it with you.

What Information Should Be Expected From the Seller of a Business?

Financial statements —(income accounts and balance sheets as a minimum) For at least three prior years, and preferably for five years.

Employee Information —Length of service, current compensation.

Tax returns —For at least three prior years, including the depreciation schedule. A buyer should never accept the excuse that the tax return pertinent to the business should be required.

Inventory and equipment list —Often this will not be prepared until after a preliminary offer or letter of intent has been made and accepted, in which case the offer should be contingent upon agreement of buyer and seller to the inventory list.

Current lists of payables and receivables—These should include aging schedules, showing the age of payables and receivables. Often not available until a letter of intent has been signed.

Customer list —(if appropriate) This can be a delicate matter, since most business sales must be handled in confidence. A seller must receive assurances that customers will not be contacted except with permission. Often not available until a letter of intent has been signed.

Interim records, ledgers and cash flow statements —To help determine seasonal fluctuations, selling patterns, cash demands, etc.

Monthly statements —Since the last annual statement was prepared to determine recent changes, if any, in the business.

Reports —Such as inspection reports, OSHA reports, plus licenses and permits.

List of key suppliers —Again, confidentiality may be essential, and the buyer can expect to be asked for assurance that suppliers will only be contacted with permission.

Diagrams and surveys—Such as septic system design, floor plans, and so forth, whenever available.

Leases & Contracts — Such as equipment, phone leases, ongoing responsibilities of business.

BUSINESS DATA FORM

Name of Business: _____

Address: _____

Owner: _____ Mailing Address: _____

Contact: _____

Data Prepared By: _____ Phone: Office _____

Date Prepared: _____ Home _____

Purpose of Evaluation/Reason for Sale: _____

SIC Code	%of Sales	SIC Code	% of Sales	SIC Code	%of Sales

SUPPORTING DATA PROVIDED

A. Financial Statements .... _____   No. of Years _____   AUDIT: Full _____

B. Tax Returns .... _____   Compilation _____

C. Depreciation Schedule .... _____   Review _____

D. Inventory of Property .... _____   L. Other (explain) _____

E. Appraisal of Real Property .... _____   _____

F. Appraisal of FF&E .... _____   _____

G. Surveys .... _____   _____

H. Business Plan .... _____   _____

I. Standard Cost Data .... _____   _____

J. Product/Service Data .... _____   _____

K. Promotional Material .... _____   _____

SHOWING SPECIFICATIONS—
INSTRUCTIONS AND KEY POINTS

_____

_____

_____

_____

_____

_____

COST OF MONEY DATA

A. Prime Rate _____

B. Prevailing Rate _____

C. Underlying Long-Term Rate _____

D. Owner Financing Available: _____

Amount _____ Rate _____

Term _____

A. ORGANIZATIONAL DATA

1. Form of organization

A. Corporation.. _____   D. Proprietorship .... _____

B. Subchapter S Corporation .... _____   E. Limited Partnership .... _____

C. Partnership...................................... _____   F. Other (explain) .... _____

2. This will be a:

A. Stock Sale .... _____   C. Other (explain) .... _____

B. Asset Sale .... _____

3. FOR CORPORATIONS ONLY:

A. Common Shares Outstanding: _____

_____

B. Other Classes Stock or Debt: _____

_____

C. Amount/Rate: _____

D. Trading Data: _____

_____

E. Shareholders: List All Major Shareholders	No. of Shares	%of Total
1.		
2.		
3.		
4.		
5.		
6.		
7.		
8.		
9.		
10.		
11.		
12.		

B. DESCRIPTIVE INFORMATION

1. History of Company:
Years in business, product change, etc. _____

_____

_____

_____

_____

_____

_____

_____

2. Description of Business:
Include photographs, note capital improvements, branches (stores or offices), etc. _____

_____

_____

_____

_____

_____

_____

3. Description of Products/Services:
Include product brochures, current price lists. _____

_____

_____

_____

_____

4. Channels of Distribution:
Number of markets being served, etc. _____

_____

_____

_____

_____

_____

5. Marketing/Sales Programs _____

_____

_____

_____

_____

_____

6. Advertising Programs:
Attach copies of recent ads, company brochure, press release articles, etc. _____

_____

_____

_____

_____

_____

_____

7. Pricing Information:
Include warranty and service policy. _____

_____

_____

_____

_____

_____

_____

8. Payment Terms _____

_____

_____

_____

_____

_____

_____

C. Sales and Market Analysis

1. Nature of Market

Area	% of Total Sales	$ Size of Total Market	Market Share %
A. Local			
B. Regional			
C. National			
D. International			

2. Market Position:

List major competitors. Quantify company strength vs. competiton. _____

_____

_____

_____

_____

_____

3. Industry Growth Rate

	Industry Growth	Company Growth
A. Past 5 Years' Average	%	%
B. Next 5 Years' Forecast	%	%

C. Source of Forecast _____

_____

4. Company Historical Sales:

Attach copies of sales tax reports if applicable. Determine real growth net of price increase.

	Total Sales	Price Increase Growth	Net Growth
A. Current Annual Sales Volume			
B. 1 Year Earlier			
C. 2 Years Earlier			
D. 3 Years Earlier			
E. 4 Years Earlier			
F. 5 Years Earlier			

5. Percent of Sales by Type

	%		%
A. One-time contract		F. Jobber/Distributor	
B. Repeat		G. Service	
C. Long-term contract		H. Route	
D. Retail		I. Mail-order	
E. Wholesale		J. Other (specify)	

6. Sales By Product Type and Gross Margin Contribution

Product Category	Sales $	%	Gross Margin Contribution $	%

7. Seasonal Sales Patterns

_____
_____
_____
_____

8. Factors Affecting Sales Forecast:

Other than straight-line projection, what factors could improve or limit growth?

_____
_____
_____
_____

D. Production/Operations

1. Production Cycle _____

_____

_____

_____

2. Capacity _____

_____

_____

_____

3. Quality Control Procedures _____

_____

_____

_____

_____

_____

4. Returned Goods Policy _____

_____

_____

_____

_____

5. Major Suppliers:

Include any special payment terms or relationships. _____

_____

_____

_____

_____

E. Facility Information
1. Conditions of Facilities

A. New, high quality .... _____

B. New, grade quality .... _____

C. Good .... _____

D. Fair .... _____

E. Poor .... _____

F. Explain _____

_____

2. Deferred Maintenance   **Remarks**

A. Item _____

Cost to Repair _____

Source of Estimate _____

B. Item _____

Cost to Repair _____

Source of Estimate _____

C. Item _____

Cost to Repair _____

Source of Estimate _____

D. Item _____

Cost to Repair _____

Source of Estimate _____

3. Maintenance Controls _____

_____

_____

_____

_____

_____

4. Estimated Value of Tangible Assets: (attach appropriate equipment inventory and schedules)

Item	Condition/Age	Market Value	Liquidation Value	Confirmed by Appraiser: Y/N
A. Land				
B. Building(s)				
C. Equipment and Machinery				
D. Furnishings (Class)				
E. Fixtures				
F. Vehicles and Rolling Stock				
G. Other Tangibles (Type)				

5. List All Tangible Assets Not Included in the Business

Description	Value	On company books Yes	No

F. Financial Data

1. Balance Sheet Information

Note any adjustments made

Current Assets

    Cash

    Inventory

    Accounts Receivable

    Other

    Total current assets

Long-term assets

    Land

    Plant

    Equipment

    Other

    Total fixed assets

    TOTAL ASSETS

Current Liabilities

    Trade payables

    Notes payable

    Other

    Total current liabilities

Long-term liabilities

    Real estate mortgage

    Other long-term liabilities

    Total Long-Term Liabilities

    TOTAL LIABILITIES

    TOTAL EQUITY

    Common Stock

    Other Equity

    Retained Earnings

2. Ratio Analysis

    A. Current ratio .... _____

    B. Quick ratio .... _____

    C. Debt to worth .... _____

    D. Inventory turns .... _____

    E. Average age of receivables .... _____

    F. Operating profit to assets (ROA) .... _____

3. Inventory: Note any difference between actual and reported

Type	Cost/Book Value	Market Value	Valuation Method	Remarks
A. Raw Materials				
B. Work in Process				
C. Completed Goods for Full-price Resale				
D. Damaged				
E. Slow-moving				
F. Marked Down				
G. Obsolete				

4. Write-Down Policy _____

_____

_____

5. Cost Accounting Procedures _____

_____

_____

6. Accounts Receivable Aging Schedule

Age	Amount	Terms
A. 0-30 Days		
B. 30-60 Days		
C. Over 90 Days		
E. Total		

7. Bad Debt, Historical Average

A. Annual Average $ _____ B. Annual Average % of Sales _____

C. Number of Years Used Above _____

8. Accounts Payable Aging Schedule

Age	Amount	Terms
A. 0-30 Days		
B. 30-60 Days		
C. 60-90 Days		
D. Over 90 Days		
E. Total		

9. Trade Debt

A. Category _____ Amount _____ Terms _____

B. Category _____ Amount _____ Terms _____

C. Category _____ Amount _____ Terms _____

D. Category _____ Amount _____ Terms _____

10. Current Debt: Attach copies of all bank notes, previous seller notes, and/or lease to be assumed

A. Lender _____ D. Amount _____

B. Loan Agreements Y/N _____ E. Term _____

C. Type _____ F. Assumable Y/N _____

A. Lender _____ D. Amount _____

B. Loan Agreements Y/N _____ E. Term _____

C. Type _____ F. Assumable Y/N _____

A. Lender _____ D. Amount _____

B. Loan Agreements Y/N _____ E. Term _____

C. Type _____ F. Assumable Y/N _____

11. Lease Information #1

A. Location _____   H. Other Terms _____

B. Use _____   I. Square Feet _____

C. Current Rates* _____   J. Condition _____

D. Percent of Gross _____   K. Utilities Paid By _____

E. Duration _____   L. Insurance Paid By _____

F. Escalation Terms _____   M. Taxes Paid By _____

G. Renewal Terms _____   N. Assignable Y/N _____

*Rate is estimated to be _____ % above _____ % below _____ average

12. Lease Information #2

A. Location _____   H. Other Terms _____

B. Use _____   I. Square Feet _____

C. Current Rates* _____   J. Condition _____

D. Percent of Gross _____   K. Utilities Paid By _____

E. Duration _____   L. Insurance Paid By _____

F. Escalation Terms _____   M. Taxes Paid By _____

G. Renewal Terms _____   N. Assignable Y/N _____

*Rate is estimated to be _____ % above _____ % below _____ average

13. Lease Information #3

A. Location _____   H. Other Terms _____

B. Use _____   I. Square Feet _____

C. Current Rates* _____   J. Condition _____

D. Percent of Gross _____   K. Utilities Paid By _____

E. Duration _____   L. Insurance Paid By _____

F. Escalation Terms _____   M. Taxes Paid By _____

G. Renewal Terms _____   N. Assignable Y/N _____

*Rate is estimated to be _____ % above _____ % below _____ average

14. Insurance

Company	Coverage Type	Cost

15. Intangible Assets (Describe) Attach materials where applicable:

A. Mailing Lists _____

_____ Estimated Value _____

B. Promotional Material _____

_____ Estimated Value _____

C. Reputation _____

_____

D. Staff _____

_____

E. Management _____

_____

F. Market Position _____

_____

G. Trademarks, Copyrights, Patents _____

_____

H. Other _____

_____

G. Labor Information: Employees

Category	Total Number	Full Time	Part Time	Seasonal	Current Salary (or range)
A. _____					
B. _____					
C. _____					
D. _____					
E. _____					
F. _____					

2. Comments: Further describe job categories, skill levels, training requirements, etc. _____

_____

_____

_____

_____

3. Union Situation

  A. Unionized .... _____

  B. Non-union .... _____

  C. Partial Union .... _____

  D. May be Unionized .... _____

4. Labor Market Characteristics: Describe availability by category _____

_____

_____

_____

5. Area Unemployment Rate _____ %   **6. Annual Workforce Turnover_____%**

7. Benefits and Policies _____

_____

_____

_____

_____

H. Management Information

1. Level of Management Skills Required (List or Comment) _____

_____

_____

_____

2. Amenities (List or Comment) _____

_____

_____

_____

3. Organizational Chart _____
_____
_____
_____
_____

I. Regulatory Information

1. Licenses Required

A. _____
B. _____
C. _____
D. _____
E. _____

2. Inspections

A. OSHA ....Date ___/___/___ Violations ....Y/N _____

B. EPA ....Date ___/___/___ Violations ....Y/N _____

C. Health Department ....Date ___/___/___ Violations ....Y/N _____

D. Fire Department ....Date ___/___/___ Violations ....Y/N _____

E. Labor Department ....Date ___/___/___ Violations ....Y/N _____

F. Explain Violations _____
_____
_____

3. Hazardous Aspects of Business _____
_____
_____
_____

4. Waste Disposal Problems (List or Comment). (Be aware of property usage over past 25 years re: hazardous waste potential.) _____
_____
_____

4. Litigation in Process or Threatened. Contingent Liability/Product Liability

_____

_____

_____

_____

J. Advisors

1. Company Attorney _____

Address _____ Telephone _____

2. Accountant _____

Address _____ Telephone _____

3. Consultants _____

Address _____ Telephone _____

4. Insurance Agent _____

Address _____ Telephone _____

5. Advertising Agency _____

Address _____ Telephone _____

6. Other _____

Address _____ Telephone _____

K. Other Information

1. Sources of Information on Industry and Company

A. Trade Publications (Name) _____

_____

B. Operations Manuals or Books (Name) _____

_____

C. Standard Cost Date (Name) _____

_____

D. Other (List) _____

_____

L. Assumptions to be used in Evaluation

1. Increased Expenses Anticipated in Forecast (Other than straight-line increases)

Item	Annual $
A. _____	_____
B. _____	_____
C. _____	_____
D. _____	_____
E. _____	_____

2. Projected Owners' Salaries

A. Job Title _____

Prevailing salary for this position in region _____ Source _____

B. Job Title _____

Prevailing salary for this position in region _____ Source _____

3. Owner Benefits Reflected in Statements to be Backed out of Projections

Item	Annual $
A. _____	_____
B. _____	_____
C. _____	_____
D. _____	_____
E. _____	_____
F. _____	_____
G. _____	_____
H. _____	_____

4. Non-Essential Assets Included in Business
(Land, Buildings, Vehicles, Equipment, Works of Art or Other Non-essential Assets)

Item	Estimated Liquidation Value
A. _____	_____
B. _____	_____
C. _____	_____
D. _____	_____

5. Non-Recurring Expenses In Historic Income Statements

	Description	Amount
1.	_____	_____
2.	_____	_____
3.	_____	_____
4.	_____	_____
5.	_____	_____
6.	_____	_____
7.	_____	_____
8.	_____	_____
9.	_____	_____

6. Special Owner Benefits to be Included In Sale

A. Living Quarters _____ Est. Annual Value: $ _____
_____

B. Insurance _____ Est. Annual Value: $ _____
_____

C. Transportation/Travel _____ Est. Annual Value: $ _____
_____

D. Food _____ Est. Annual Value: $ _____
_____

E. Wholesale Purchases _____ Est. Annual Value: $ _____
_____

F. Living Expenses _____ Est. Annual Value: $ _____
_____

G. Expense Account _____ Est. Annual Value: $ _____
_____

H. Pension/IRA, etc. _____ Est. Annual Value: $ _____
_____

I. Tax Shelter _____ Est. Annual Value: $ _____

Estimated Total Annual Value of Benefits: $ _____

Business Inventory Checklist

The purpose of this form is to help you spot areas of your business which need to be improved. If you find a significant number of check marks against either the "NO" or "?" column on the right of the form, you should at least ask yourself whether it would pay off to devote specific detailed attention to these areas. Please note that the Business Inventory Checklist corresponds in content with the Skills Inventory Checklist on page 21.

I. Sales and Marketing

Item	Consideration	Yes	No	?	Notes
		Based upon my analysis of the business, I believe that the operation is currently being run satisfactorily.			
A. Pricing	Is markup in line with current industry practice and/or competition so that there is a reasonable profit?				
B. Market Research	Has the business taken advantage of market potential? Has competition been analyzed?				
C. Personal Selling	Does Current management use good honest selling techniques?				
D. Customer Service	Is there proper balance between serving the customers' needs and good business practice?				
E. Advertising and	Does the business spend enough in advertising and promotion? Does the amount spent make sense with the level of business and its growth? Are results measured?				
F. Sales Management	Are Salespersons and outside agents properly directed in their duties?				
G. Market Planning	Has the business taken advantage of market opportunities? Is the business benefiting from trends in the market?				

II. Business Operations

Item	Consideration	Yes	No	?	Notes
A. Purchasing	Are reputable, competitive vendors used? Is there a purchasing "program"?				
B. Inventory Control	Is slow-moving stock (or materials) under control? How does inventory turnover compare to industry averages?				
C. Scheduling	Do goods and materials move through the business without tie-ups and problems?				
D. Quality Control	Are inferior incoming materials sent back to the suppliers? Are customers satisfied with the current products?				
	Does the company have to contend with cheap, discount competition? Can quality be maintained or improved?				
E. Business Growth	Has the business grown at least equal to the rate of inflation? Is demand expected to rise or fall in the next decade?				
F. Insurance	Are risks to the business properly covered?				

III. Financial

Item	Consideration	Yes	No	?	Notes
A. Bookkeeping and Accounting	Are the books of the company adequate? Are records easy to come by?				
B. Budgeting	Is a cash flow budget used?				
C. Cost Control	Are cost items managed and efforts applied to items of high cost to keep them under control?				

III. Financial (Continued)

Item	Consideration	Yes	No	?	Notes
D. Raising Money	Has the current owner(s) been successful in raising borrowed funds or equity capital when it was needed?				
E. Credit and Collection	Is the current Credit and Collection policy adequate for today's needs?				
F. Dealing with Banks	Is the relationship between the business owner and banker open and friendly?				
G. Credit Management	When loans were taken out, were the interest rate and the loan conditions appropriate?				
H. Specific Areas	Are accurate data available on: 1. Break-even level? 2. Cash flow? 3. Financial statements? 4. Operating ratios? 5. Tax planning?				

IV. Personal

Item	Consideration	Yes	No	?	Notes
A. Hiring	Has the right mix of people been hired? Is turnover under control?				
B. Training	Are the employees suitably trained for what they are expected to do?				
C. Motivating People	Do the employees appear to enjoy what they are doing?				
D. Enforcing Policies	Do there seem to be logic and order to what goes on in the business?				
E. Communication	Do employees know what is going on? Are they brought in on decisions?				

V. Administrative/Management

Item	Consideration	Yes	No	?	Notes
A. Record Keeping	Are records of past transactions and events kept so that they are easy to find?				
B. Problem Solving	Have problem areas been identified? Have plans been developed to solve these problems?				
C. Decision Making	Is the current owner able to make prompt, satisfactory decisions?				
E. Leadership	Is the current owner really in charge of the business and its employees?				
F. Business Law	Does the company have a substantial legal exposure (e.g. to product liability suits)? Is there pending or expected litigation? Are legal files (e.g. of contracts) in order?				
G. Dealing with Professionals	Does the business have and use a knowledgeable accountant, attorney, or consultant? Can you use them also?				

Summary

Acquiring and analyzing data is so important in managing a small business successfully that Step Seven, Effective Use of Information Resources, is part of the acquisition method we recommend.

The Business Data Form helps you identify and organize the information about the business you are interested in acquiring. It isn't intended to cover everything—there will be qualitative aspects of the business that affect your decision—but it does provide a framework.

Don't rush through this step. The quality of your acquisition decision is affected by the quality of the investigative efforts you put in beforehand. A high level of attention to these important details will pay off handsomely.

Step Three:
Proper Acquisition Price and Terms

CASE IN POINT

Placing a value on a business with consolidated financial records adds difficulties to the already tough task of determining the value of a going business. When Serafino "Skee" Fusco and his brother-in-law Bob Busch finally found the right manufacturing business for their plans, National Fiber Insulation (Amherst, Massachusetts), the financial records and assets were consolidated with two other businesses.

Before they were through, they had generated three separate sets of best-case, worst-case, and most-likely-case income projections. A list of the business assets for National Fiber was developed, but as is often the case, the replacement cost bore no resemblance to the book value. Dic Molari, the CBI associate working with Mr. Fusco and Mr. Busch, established that the value of the assets should correspond to the "in-place value" of the equipment —the replacement cost of comparable used equipment plus installation.

Once the asset value and working capital requirements of a company are determined and the actual profitability known, a business value can be equitably established by combining the value of the assets with normal financial rates of return. This is the first step: now terms and the form of the sale have to be structured in. Whether to structure the transaction as a stock or an asset sale, how to treat outstanding accounts receivable, what to do with employment and consulting contracts will become much easier to negotiate once the basic valuation is agreed upon.

With National Fiber, a compromise was made by the buyers for a slightly higher price based on the sellers' agreement to an asset sale. This negotiation produced the kind of win-win situation that CBI always tries to achieve, a transaction that makes good sense for both buyer and seller.

Determining the current value of a business is essential before you begin the process of negotiating price and terms. The *price* is a function of the *value* of the business (what you are willing to pay for it) and the *terms* of the transaction (the structure of the financing, including down payment, timing and amounts of subsequent payments, tax liabilities and other negotiable considerations). Prices are flexible. It may be that a higher price spread over a longer term is more favorable for you than a lower price due up front. It depends on you, the business, the seller, and current tax laws.

Business value is based on several factors: the value of the tangible assets involved; the earning power of the business; the internal and external factors that could affect this earning power; future prospects and risks; the desirability of the business and more. The value of a business is normally based on historical and current years' performance. The major benefit of future years' earnings belongs to the buyer not the seller. It helps to separate out the value of the business as a going concern (the subject of this step) from the value of the business as you plan to view it (the subject of Step Four). You have to have some idea of what you will do with the business over the next three years in order to understand what level of debt and risk you will accept. This is a classic chicken and egg situation: you need to know price and terms to write a business plan, but you need the business plan to negotiate price and terms!

If you think you can increase earnings dramatically (increased capital, new techniques, better marketing or whatever), the business might be worth more to you and you can loosen up a bit on terms. This doesn't mean the business is intrinsically more valuable. It means that you have more freedom in establishing the structure of the sale. On the other hand, if it looks as if the earnings will decline, the business is worth less to you, and may be less valuable intrinsically as well if the earnings trend is indeed down.

Experience shows that although some cost ordinarily can be reduced in the first year or so, earnings tend to remain steady until you have time to effect changes. Consequently, it is more constructive to project next year on the basis of the current performance. Momentum is always harder to redirect than we think it will be.

When you buy a business you should also buy positive cash flow that will help pay for the business over the course of the negotiated terms. As a result, if you have (let's suppose) $100,000 to invest in a business, you may find that you can purchase a business worth many times that sum. The determinants are the structure of the transaction, including price and terms of the financing, the projections of future stabilized earnings including the cost necessary to achieve the projections (*your* projections for two or three years out, based on your plans and assumptions, not the seller's), and the amount of risk you and your financing sources are willing to bear.

Use of the business's ability to generate cash flow is one of the great attractions of purchasing a going business as contrasted with starting a business from scratch. However, determining what that cash flow will be under uncertain future conditions is far from simple. It starts with establishing a value (as opposed to price) for the business, based on careful scrutiny of the assets and earning power of the business as currently operated.

This section lists the basic steps involved in business evaluation. Although you can use this to arrive at a reasonably accurate estimated value, it is very important to note that business evaluation calls for more expertise than may at first be obvious.

To protect yourself, get professional assistance. A qualified business broker will normally have prepared a detailed evaluation of any company he or she is representing. Brokers usually represent the seller on a confidential basis, and will not hand out information indiscriminately. If you have a genuine interest in the business, and if you are financially qualified, the broker will share the evaluation and explain the research, appraisals and assumptions used in recommending price and terms.

If the business is *not* represented by a certified business broker, you will have a more difficult task ahead. The appraisals and assumptions used by the seller (or the seller's agents) need to be substantiated and critically evaluated. How was the price determined? What terms is the seller prepared to offer? How can you make a rational, businesslike judgment on these matters if you are not used to evaluating such transactions?

This section provides an example plus a comprehensive Business Evaluation Form to help you reach an independent evaluation. While the form provides a rational framework for discussion of the value placed on the business, it must be noted that ultimately the test of what the business is worth is a marketing judgment: what will a buyer —you—actually pay for the business? Approach the valuation process with this in mind. These are guidelines, not Gospel, for the following reasons:

- The inventory and working capital (funds needed to finance the inventory) requirements are difficult to determine under the best of circumstances. You should consider the average level of inventory (not necessarily the same as shown in the year-end statement, since inventories usually will have seasonal fluctuations), as well as an analysis of accounts payable and accounts receivable cash flows. Add to this questions concerning the age and quality of receivables and inventories, and the need for outside advice becomes (we hope) clear.

- The valuation of tangible assets (land, buildings, and equipment) is difficult. Professional appraisers spend years acquiring the expertise to properly assess the value of property, and spend much of their professional lives keeping up to date with fluctuating tangible asset values.

- Valuation of intangible assets is even more difficult, as it depends on accurate and timely knowledge of local and regional market and economic conditions, competitive factors, and availability of financing. The section on Intangible Business Value (see page 77 below) is another area where objective skills are required. The knowledge of market conditions and their interplay with internal and external factors which might affect growth is not easily gained. Bankers, consultants, and other experts may be of some use here, if they have experience in this form of analysis.

- Analyzing and understanding the external and internal factors that could influence earnings is essential—and also calls for professional, objective assistance. It is unlikely that an amateur or beginner, no matter how gifted, could arrive at realistic values on which to base negotiations.

- The value placed on goodwill must reflect excess earnings (a problem in and of itself); cash flow to cover the proposed debt, fair salary for the owner, and replacement of fixed assets; provide a return on the invested cash; and provide a return on the assets purchased. Goodwill is not the same as potential, or what the seller thinks might happen if only everything works out well. Unhappily, many sellers don't understand this, and even fewer understand the impact that the valuation of goodwill can have on the structure of the transaction.

- The **structure** of the transaction—the negotiated final price, terms, and legal and tax agreements—dramatically impacts the potential success of your venture. Most small business acquisitions involve a combination of bank and seller financing in addition to the cash down payment. You will need the services of a competent tax lawyer and accountant to make sure that the legal and tax angles are covered, and must be confident that the cash flow from the business will be strong enough to pay down the financing. The seller, particularly if he or she is providing financing, will often accommodate terms to the cash flow.

- Negotiating terms is immensely complex. Get the best professional help you can find; get an experienced business broker or consultant who has been involved in many other business transfers on your team of professionals; and leave the negotiations to them. While you have to make critical decisions about the amount you can invest, what terms you can live with, and what level of debt you feel you can shoulder, remember that you don't enter into these valuation and negotiation processes more than once or twice in your lifetime.

Some of the variables in the final structure include tax considerations, use of consulting or other contracts as part of the transfer of value, use of seller financing (where the seller takes back paper as a key piece of the financing), timing of payments, discounting accounts receivable, handling debt, contingent liabilities, and literally thousands of other potential considerations.

If this sounds somewhat daunting to you, good. It should. If a lawyer who represents himself has a fool for a client, so does a business buyer. In no part of the acquisition process is relying on competent professional advice more important.

With that understood, use the following form to establish a sense of the value of the business you are thinking of acquiring.

Summary
The first set of forms helped you establish a range of values for the business under consideration. While it is somewhat subjective, it helps define areas of agreement (as well as disagreement) with the seller.

The Business Evaluation Form is more precise, and reflects the value of the business as a going concern. It helps you estimate the most likely performance of the business over the next year, spells out the investment needed to fund the purchase and generation of the business, and provides some important financial information for your lenders and other interested parties.

The completed Business Evaluation Form provides an accurate, well-based assessment of the value of the business as currently operated. This, in turn, is the basis for negotiation on price and terms.

A Business Should Yield Three Forms of Returns To an Owner:

1. Owner's salary for time spent managing and/or operating.

2. Return to fund the purchase of the business assets

3. Return on investment—amount of money invested by buyer.

Basic Procedure for Evaluation

Below is a brief summary of the evaluation process. The more detailed outline which follows will clarify some of the many adjustments required for an accurate evaluation.

Step	Example
1. Determine current market value of tangible assets of the business.	Asset value = $190,000 (+ inventory of $60,000)
2. Determine the most probable earning power of the business—before interest and after making various adjustments outlined below—for 12 months, beginning on date of evaluation.	$44,450
3. Establish the appropriate rate of return for the investment in tangible assets (1).	Bank prime rate + 2%
4. Multiply (1) by (3) to determine "cost of money" as defined on form.	.12 x $250.000
5. Subtract (4) from (2) to determine "excess earning power."	$44,450 – $30,000 = $14,450
6. Select an appropriate multiple (see form) for "excess earnings." For this example, use 4.8 as the multiple to determine value of "excess earnings."-	Multiple chosen using form is 4.8 4.8 x $14,450 (excess earning power) = $69,360
7. Add the value of "excess earnings" as shown in (6) above to the value of the tangible assets, (1) above. This is the indicated value of the business.	$190,000 + $69,360 = $259,360 Value = $260,000 + inventory

Following are suggestions to follow for each of the seven steps listed above.

1. Determine Current Market Value of Tangible Assets.

Tangible Fixed Assets, including the following, should be appraised at fair market value.

Real Estate   Source: real estate appraiser

Furniture and Fixtures   Source: office furniture dealer

Machinery   Source: used machinery dealer

Vehicles   Source: NADA publication

2. Determine Probable Earning Power

Establish a time frame

◆   Project probable income and expense during your first year of ownership. Be sure to pick a time frame consistent with the business' fiscal year, e.g. if the business is on a calendar year and you are reviewing it in the first six months, the owner's forecast for the current year might provide the basis. However, if you are looking at the business in the last six months, you should first develop a forecast for the current year (based on 6 months actual and 6 months forecast), and then your own projections for the next 12 months, remembering that it could take 3-4 months or longer before you actually buy the business.

Determine factors which will affect performance

◆   inflation
◆   improvements in the business made by present owner, i.e. added manufacturing capacity or new rooms, or product lines in previous year

Project sales and expenses for 12 months

◆   substitute an "asset replacement fund" for depreciation (if in doubt, put in as an expense about 1/8 the value of furnishings, fixtures and equipment)
◆   determine owner's salary
◆   eliminate former owner's personal benefits
◆   check expense items with "standard industry costs" to see that they are adequate (see bibliography)
◆   eliminate interest cost (to be done later)

Examples of adjustments used to "stabilize" income account:

Adjusting Earnings

Item	1990 Per Tax Return	1991 Pro Forma 1st Yr. Owner	+ or -	Explanation
Sales	$460,000	$525,000	+$65,000 +14.1%	Trade association forecasts @ 10% annual growth for the next five years. Increased contracts already received = $18,000.
Cost of Sales	344,000	393,000	+$49,000 +14%	Assumption that variable cost will remain at 75% of sales.
Advertising	6,300	14,200	+$7,900 +125%	Establish variable cost budget of 2.7% of sales. Reference, Robert Morris Assoc. Former budget unrealistic.
Insurance	3,850	14,200	+$7,900 +125%	Based on current estimate supplied by underwriter reflecting new valuations.
Utilities	3,450	4,600	+$1,150 +33%	Fuel & electric rates estimated up 52%. Inexpensive conservation measures should keep within estimate.
Overhead	16,000	18,000	+$2,000 +12.2%	Anticipated raises to present staff. No additional help needed for anticipated increase in sales.

Calculate Indicated Profit

Example:

Sales...$		525,000
Cost of Sales		-393,000
Gross profit ....$		132,000
Operating and Administrative Expenses		-87,550
Indicated Profit ....$		44,450

3. Establish Appropriate Rate of Returns, and

4. Determine "Cost of Money"

The cost of money is a dollar amount which is calculated using the required rate of return for tangible assets. Multiply the rate of return used by the value of tangible assets plus required working capital to get the cost of money.

One indication of the required rate of return for tangible business assets is the current bank prime rate plus 2%.

Example:

Tangible Assets ....$		190,000
Extra Working Capital Needs...		+60,000
Total ....$		250,000
Required Rate of return for Tangible Assets		12%
Cost of Money ....$		30,000

5. Determining "Excess Earnings"

Determine how much is left over after deducting cost of money from probable earnings

Indicate Profit .... $	44,450
Cost of Money	-30,000
Excess Earnings	14,450

6. Calculate a Multiplier for "Excess Earnings" (Scale of 0 to 60)

Example: (Based on the Business Evaluation Form at the end of this section). This is subjective but has proven itself in the market place through years of consistent use. An article published by Harvard Business Review on this approach is included in the back of this book. It is in this area that the experience of a qualified business broker is essential. They understand the market.

Factor	Comments	Value
Risk	In business 22 years; high repeat business; no cyclicality; business growth virtually assured by market	5
	Owner will give extensive help and training	
	Owner will guarantee accounts receivable and adjust inventory downward	
Competitive situation	Market far from saturated; relatively high cost of entry discourages competition.	6
Industry	Standard & Poor's indicates growth through 1990 of over 10 percent in constant dollars from home-related business other than new constructions	4
Company	Well-established, many years of profitability	5
	Excellent records	
	Good management systems	

Factors	Comments	Value
Company Growth	Company growth has been about equal to the industries it is a part of	4
	Several programs started to expand base, some of which are promising	
Desirability	Very pleasant business in a nice environment	5
	Moderate status and challenge	
	Special benefits average for a business this size; includes living quarters on second floor at low conversion cost	
	Total rating	29
	Multiplier (divided by 6)	4.8

7. Calculate Market Value By Adding Value of Excess Earnings to Market Value of Tangible Assets

Example:

1.	Extra Earnings	$	14,450
2.	Multiplier		4.8
3.	Value of Extra Earnings	$	69,360
4.	Add Asset Value	$	190,000
5.	Market Value	$	259,360
6.	Rounded to	$	260,000

The Business Evaluation Form

In using the **Business Evaluation Form**, you will need to make various adjustments to each income and expense entry. For example, if fuel oil costs have been rising rapidly, you will have to make a substantial adjustment to the expenses incurred in the last year. If the owner has a large personal following of customers, you may have to spend more on advertising to sustain the business. Your insurance cost may go up.

There may be other costs which don't belong in a "stabilized" earnings statement—for example, extra-high cost because the owner was sick for a period of time, or some other expense that reflected the present owner's style more than the substance of the business.

You will need to enter an appropriate owner's salary where indicated. This should be the amount you would have to pay someone else competent to do the work involved in managing the business.

You will also need to eliminate the item on past income statements for depreciation and substitute an amount of money that, if put aside each year, would allow you to buy new equipment, furnishings and fixtures as they wear out in future years.

Do not include interest expense until you arrive at the section for determining "cost of money." Be certain to include "cost of money" for the entire value of the fixed assets of the business, not just for the part you intend to borrow.

In preparing the stabilized income account (lines 1 to 23), you are attempting to show the most likely performance for the business owner the ensuing 12-month period. Don't use projections from your own business plan projections, which may include changes you would make in the business. This should be a picture of the business with the strengths and weaknesses it has at present—this is what you pay for when you buy a business.

You may need to have an appraisal done of the business real estate and other assets such as furnishings, fixtures and equipment. An accurate estimate of asset value is essential in determining business value.

Follow the form closely for each item and it will lead to a reasonably accurate conclusion about the value of the business.

Having established the value of the business the form guides you through certain financing assumptions (down payment, bank, and seller) so that the ability to purchase establishes the return on investment, and the business and the financing assumptions are identified.

Business Evaluation Form

Name of Business _____

_____

Address _____

_____

Contact _____

_____

Data Prepared By _____

_____

Date Prepared _____

_____

Approved By _____ Date: _____

Purpose of Evaluation _____

_____

_____

_____

Major Assumptions Used in Evaluation _____

_____

_____

_____

_____

_____

Pro Forma Profit and Loss Analysis

Sales

Previous Year
(2 or 3)
Year Ending

1. Net sales	After sales tax, discounts, and returns		100%

Cost of Sales

2. Beginning Inventory			
3. Purchases	Including raw materials, operating supplies, freight		
4. Operating Labor	Not including Overhead Labor shown on Line 16		
5. Sub Total			
6. Ending Inventory			
7. Cost of Sales	Line 6 minus Line 5		
8. Gross Profit	Line 7 minus Line 1		

Expenses

9. Accounting, Consulting, Legal			
10. Advertising and Promotion			
11. Employee Benefits			
12. Heat, Light, Power	Type of Heat:		
13. Insurance			
14. Office Supplies & Expense			
15. Operating Supplies	Operating and maintenance supplies not included in Cost of Goods, Line 3		
16. Overhead Labor	Including office and sales staff. Not including owner-manager or Operating Labor, Line 4		
17. Taxes/Fees/Licenses	Including payroll taxes, real estate taxes, other		
18. Telephone, Photocopier, Fax			
19. Transportation, Auto, travel			
20. Rent			
21. Other Expenses			

Expenses (continued)

22.	Owner's Salary	Adjusted to reflect value of special benefits		
23.	Maintenance & Repairs	Annual amount to maintain all assets adequately		
24.	Reserve for Replacement	Average annual amount sufficient to replace assets as they wear out		
25.	Reserve for Contingencies			
26.	Total Expenses	Total Lines 9 through 26		
27.	Operating Income	Line 8 minus Line 26		

Previous Year ____ (2 or 1) Year Ending ____		Previous Year ____ (1, or 2 yr. avg.) Year Ending ____		Pro Forma		
				Month ____ Actual	Month ____ Projection	12 Month ____ Pro Forma

Tangible Assets and Working Capital Requirements

28. Market Value of Real Estate	Land and buildings reflecting cost of deferred maintenance and required repairs
29. Market Value of Other Tangible Assets	Including furnishings, fixtures, machinery
30. Inventory & Working Capital Requirements	Average Cost of Inventory $ _____ Funding Accounts Receivable _____ Subtotal _____ Minus Accounts Payable (_____) Plus Estimate Additional W/C _____ Working Capital Requirement _____
31. Total Tangible Asset Value Plus Working Capital Requirements	
32. Capitalization Rate Applicable	Land and buildings % x ____ = ___ % FF & E % x ____ = ___ % Inventory % x ____ = ___ % Applicable Capitalization Rate _____ %
33. Annual Cost of Money	

Adjusted Earnings

34. Operating Income	Re-enter Line 27	
35. Annual Cost of Money	Re-enter Line 33	
36. Adjusted or Excess Earnings	Line 27 minus Line 33	

Intangible Business Value

37. Risk Rating (between 0 and 6)	0—Continuity of income at risk 3—Steady income likely 6—Growing income assured
38. Competitive Rating (between 0 and 6)	0—Highly competitive in unstable market 3—Normal competitive conditions 6—Dynamic industry, rapid growth likely
40. Company Rating (between 0 and 6)	0—Recent start-up, not established 3—Well established, satisfactory track record 6—Long record of sound operation, outstanding reputation

41. Company Growth Rating (between 0 and 6)	0—Business has been declining 3—Steady growth, slightly faster than inflation rate 6—Dynamic growth rate	
42. Desirability Rating (between 0 and 6)	0—No status, rough or dirty work 3—Respected business in satisfactory environment 6—Challenging business in attractive environment	
43. Total Ranking	Sum of Lines 37 through 42	
44. Multiple	Line 43 divided by 6	
45. Adjusted or Excess Earnings	Re-enter Line 36	
46. Intangible Business Value	Line 44 multiplied by Line 45	

Total of Tangible Assets and Intangible Business Value

47. Total Asset Value	Line 28 plus Line 29	
48. Intangible Business Value	Re-enter Line 46	
49. **Total Business Value**	Line 47 plus Line 48 not including inventory	

Projected Annual Earnings For Owner of the Business

50. TOTAL INVESTMENT	Line 49 plus Line 30, Working Capital Requirements	
51. Down Payment		

52. Balance to be financed

Amount	Years	Type	Rate	Monthly Payments	Total Payments First Year

Total Payments First Year $ _____

53. First year principal portion only of 52		
54. Operating income	Re-enter Line 27.	

55.	Annual Debt Service	Re-enter Line 52	
56.	Pre-tax Business Cash Flow	Line 54 minus Line 5	
57.	Principal Payment	Re-enter Line 53	
58.	Pre-tax Equity Income	Line 56 plus Line 57	

59.	DepreciationValue	Life	Type	Amount first year
	A. Real estate			
	B. Furniture, Fixtures			
	C. Equipment			
	D. Consulting Non-Competition Agreements			
	E. Total Depreciation/ Amortization			
	F. Excess Over Replacement Fund	Line 59E less line 23		

60.	Taxable Income	Line 58 less line 59F	
61.	Estimated Tax Credits		
62.	Estimated Business Taxes		
63.	After-Tax Business Income	Line 60 less line 62	
64.	After-Tax Business Cash Flow	Line 56 less line 62	
65.	Owners' salaries	From line 22	

Description	Amount

66.	Spendable Income Before Personal Tax	Line 64 plus Line 65	
67.	After-Tax Equity Income	Line 58 less Line 62	
68.	After Tax Return on Total Investment	$\dfrac{\text{Operating income (Line 27)}}{\text{Total investment (Line 50)}}$	%
69.	After-Tax Return on Investment	$\dfrac{\text{After tax equity income (Line 67)}}{\text{Down payment (Line 51)}}$	%

Key Financial Data

A. Fiscal Year End _____

B. Average Accounts Receivable Balance _____

Days Outstanding A/R _____

C. Average Accounts Payable Balance _____

Days Outstanding A/P _____

D. Raw Material Inventory _____ Method

Work in Process Inventory _____ Method

Finished Goods Inventory _____ Method

Total Inventory _____

E. Land Value _____ Source _____ Date _____

F. Buildings Value _____ Source _____ Date _____

G. Equipment Value _____ Source _____ Date _____

H. FF&E _____ Source _____ Date _____

I. List of Key Employees

	Hourly		Monthly		Weekly	
Position	Number	Date	Number	Date	Number	Date

J. Existing Leases	Description	Term	Amount	Options

Step Four:
A Reasonable and
Complete Business Plan

CASE IN POINT

Spectacular location and awesome natural beauty aren't the only assets of The Black Bear Inn in Bolton Valley, Vermont. "This inn is an outstanding property as far as financial performance goes," says Ed Kiniry, CBI's chairman and an associate based in the Burlington Office. "Since the only way to succeed in this business is by offering guests the right ambiance, the right food and the right kinds of comforts, an innkeeper has to be on top of what's happening in the business, in the market and in the industry. I have never seen a better system for information management than the one at the Black Bear Inn."

Ed first became involved with the inn when it was sold by CBI to Phil and Sue McKinnis in 1982. "Despite excellent jobs—I was controller for a $30 million division of Emerson Electric and Sue was an executive chef who'd trained at hotel management school, we just weren't happy" Phil explains, When a friend from Wall Street told me to take a relaxing vacation at a New England country inn, I started thinking about buying one instead. With my financial management skills and Sue's culinary skills, I thought we'd be quite a team.

"Over one long weekend in 1982, I put a business plan together, Sue studied the operation, and we gave Ed our letter of intent. When our offer was accepted, we rushed back to St. Louis to quit our jobs and prepare to move to Vermont."

When Phil and Sue actually took over operations, the inn was full and they served 40 people for dinner their first night. Sue refers to their tenure as "the dinner party that lasted eight years." They worked long, hard days and stuck to their plan of making improvements in stages. "The McKinneses took what had been a ski lodge," Ed explains, "and turned it into a country inn. In addition to their commitment, what really helped them achieve their goals was their disciplined management system. Phil developed software so he could always have accurate, up-to-date information. He knew everything about the Inn's bookings, and where and when to run ads. If an ad wasn't pulling, he knew exactly what to do."

The business planning process is the most important activity you will conduct in preparing for the acquisition of a small business.

If you are unfamiliar with the business planning process, we strongly recommend that you buy a copy of the *Business Planning Guide* (BPG). The BPG is a complete workbook that takes you through the planning process, provides a running example and illustrates what may be unfamiliar concepts. The BPG contains worksheets for your convenience and will make the very important planning task far simpler. (See the bibliography in Step Seven for ordering information.)

A complete, thorough business plan helps you to formulate strategies for operating the business by showing how all of the parts of the business (and its products and markets) fit together. You can compare a business plan to a map: it helps you get from where you are to where you are eager to go and allows for alternate routes. And like a map, it is only useful if it is followed.

On the following pages an outline of a business plan is shown. Preparing a plan takes time, especially in the case of a business new to you (even if you are experienced in the line of business, a new acquisition poses many unfamiliar problems.) The effort you put into the preparation will be amply rewarded in many ways:

1.   The process of writing the business plan helps you spot trouble beforehand (and helps you avoid or diminish many problems);

2.   as you write down the business plan, you will gain a more comprehensive picture of your own skills and the skills of those persons available to you (family, bankers, advisors, employees);

3.   as obstacles present themselves in the plan, you will be devising new solutions, identifying strengths and discerning new applications for old products and processes, and in general bringing order to the difficult task of managing a small business;

4.   your plan will keep your business efforts focused on achieving measurable results that are directly tied to your goals. Lack of such focus is the single greatest danger small business owners must contend with. Just as a map helps you select a path across the desert and reach your destination before you run out of water, your business plan helps you achieve your goals without wasting resources and running out of cash. It is the key to avoiding the most common reason for business failure, the lack of adequate capitalization.

Just having clearly defined goals (the basis of your business plan) will set your enterprise apart from the average small business. Most small businesses are run reactively, responding to outside pressures and crises, repeating the same errors time and again. By defining your goals, you create some fixed points (think of the map analogy) that help you measure progress, assess performance on a consistent basis, and gradually improve operations.

That's the biggest payoff. Your business has to provide you with enough information to make sure that operations are running as planned. Without a written business plan, the only way to succeed is to trust to experience and luck. With a written plan, the approach is more systematic: goals and time parameters are established, the means of measuring progress—or the lack of it—are built into the daily business activities, and the resulting feedback helps you manage the business rather than being managed by factors outside your control.

Where do you start a plan? By defining clearly what the business is; that is, making a model in words and numbers of the business as you would like to see it. The written business plan helps you to focus your thinking, and the resulting model stands to the business as the map stands to the geography: some high points and landmarks are used as reference points to help guide you, while less important details are eliminated. The stunt that is hard for cartographers and business planners is deciding what details to keep in, what specifics to include or omit, and what scale to use.

As you proceed with the planning process, you will probably need some help. Business plans (according to our experience) are written in uneven lumps: a few ideas are jotted down on an envelope, another vagrant thought on a yellow pad, and sooner or later all the loose pieces are pulled together. Don't try to rush the process. A business plan takes a lot of thought and consideration, and by allowing your ideas to mature a bit you will always benefit. You may have to have some professional assistance for the financial and other technical sections. However, in the long run you, and you alone, have to be able to understand and articulate every detail and assumption in your business plan, so it is a good idea to be thoroughly involved in the entire process.

A three-ring binder with dividers makes planning somewhat easier. Planning is not a linear process: one day you might work on the marketing or product section, another time on personnel, yet another on who the competitors are and what they are doing. Periodic reviews of your plan will give you a sense of what is still needed and as a dividend will sharpen your sense of how you like to spend your own time. Keep your notes and ideas for future reference. Even after you have finished your plan, this material can be useful.

Your completed business plan is your best possible financing proposal. It details what you plan to do, how you plan to accomplish those specific goals, what management skills and personnel will be brought to bear, what the market prospects are and a thousand other considerations. A good technique is to get your banker involved. Bankers (like all of us) enjoy using their best skills, and since financial management is apt to be a problem in many small businesses you gain doubly: your banker will help you avoid financial mistakes (seeking the wrong kind of financing, taking undue risks, trying to stretch a small amount of capital too far) while at the same time making it tough to turn down the request for financing that he or she has just finished assembling with you.

Summary

Your business plan is, above all else, a communications tool for employees and investors, bankers and vendors, and even for yourself. Running a business is an extraordinarily complex job. Your plan helps you set priorities, making sure that all parts of the business are pursuing the same goals, and over time will help you maximize the use of your business resources. For the investment, you can't beat it.

Business planning doesn't end with the completion of a written draft. Circumstances change, competition comes and goes, markets shift, and your own goals will change as well. As an astute business owner, update your business plan periodically, at least annually (and certainly no more often than quarterly) and consult it often. Your plan is a tool that must be used to be useful.

After the acquisition, your business plan will help you manage the transition smoothly. Share it. It will keep you on course, help you avoid making unnecessary and possibly hazardous changes, and reassure the suppliers and employees who will be understandably concerned about your new management. Ask them for ideas; this can only strengthen your business and your skills.

The Importance of a Good Business Plan

◆ You need a business plan to purchase and operate a business.

◆ Your financing source will need to see your business plan to see where you are going and what it will take to get there.

◆ Your business plan gives a definite direction to the business.

◆ A business plan forces you to work out a financial structure in advance and makes you think through expected future developments.

◆ Your business plan will make you aware of opportunities and prevent over-reaction to problems.

◆ A business plan increases the probability of success in a venture and improves as it is tested against experience.

Suggested Outline of Business Plan

- Cover Sheet: Name of business, names of principals, address and phone number of business

_____

_____

_____

_____

_____

- Statement of purpose _____

_____

_____

_____

_____

- Table of contents _____

_____

_____

_____

_____

_____

I. The Business

A. Description of business: Include your mission statement: What business are you really in? What is the purpose of the Business

Notes: _____

_____

_____

_____

_____

B. **Products and Services:** Include a brief description of the markets your products and services will be sold to. Consider how these products may change over the planning period.

Notes: _____

_____

_____

_____

_____

_____

_____

_____

_____

_____

C. **Location of Business:** Why is the location right (or wrong) for this business.

Notes: _____

_____

_____

_____

_____

_____

_____

D. **Management:** Who does what?

Notes _____

_____

_____

_____

_____

_____

_____

_____

E. **Personnel**

Notes: _____

_____

_____

_____

_____

_____

_____

_____

_____

_____

II. The Marketing Plan

A. **Markets Served:** Who are current and prospective customers?

Notes: _____

_____

_____

_____

_____

B. **Demographics of Market:** What are the individuals in these markets like? (Age, sex, income, or buying patterns and so forth.)

Notes: _____

_____

_____

_____

_____

_____

C. **Position in Market:** How do you compare with others?

Notes: _____

_____

_____

   1. Price

   Notes: _____

_____

   2. Quality

   Notes: _____

_____

   3. Other

   Notes: _____

_____

D. **Competition:**

Notes: _____

_____

E. **Trends in the Market:**

Notes: _____

_____

F. **Share of Market:** Analysis and Projections

Notes: _____

_____

_____

III. Financial Data

A. Sources and Applications of Funding

Notes: _____

_____

_____

_____

_____

_____

_____

_____

_____

B. Capital Equipment and Capital Improvement List

Notes: _____

_____

_____

_____

_____

_____

_____

_____

_____

_____

C. Opening Balance Sheet

Notes: _____

_____

_____

_____

_____

D. Break-even Analysis

Notes: _____

_____

_____

_____

_____

_____

_____

_____

E. Income Projections (Profit and Loss Statements)

1. Three-year summary

Notes: _____

_____

_____

_____

_____

_____

_____

_____

2. Detail by month for first year

Notes: _____

_____

_____

_____

_____

_____

3. Detail by quarter for second and third years

Notes: _____

_____

_____

_____

4. Notes of explanation

Notes: _____

_____

_____

_____

_____

_____

F. Pro-Forma Cash Flow

1. Detail by month for first year

Notes: _____

_____

_____

_____

_____

_____

_____

_____

2. Detail by quarter for second and third years

Notes: _____

_____

_____

_____

_____

_____

3. Notes of explanation

Notes: _____

_____

_____

G. Budget and Format for Deviation Analysis

Notes: _____

_____

_____

_____

_____

_____

_____

_____

H. Historical Financial Reports for Existing Business

1. Balance sheets for past three years

Notes: _____

_____

_____

_____

_____

_____

_____

_____

_____

2. Income statements for past three years

Notes: _____

_____

_____

_____

_____

_____

3. Tax returns

Notes: _____

_____

_____

IV. Supporting Documents:

Personal resumes, personal financial requirements and statements, credit reports, letters of reference, job descriptions, product or service literature, photographs of real estate or products, letters of intent, copies of leases, contracts, legal documents, and anything else of relevance to the plan.

Notes: _____

_____

_____

_____

_____

_____

_____

_____

_____

_____

_____

_____

Step Five:
Adequate Capitalization

CASE IN POINT

"We've seen how important having adequate capital is," explains Jeff Hagstrom. "During our first month as new owners, most of the checks that came in were for the previous owners, not for us. If we didn't have our line of credit, we'd have been in big trouble."

Jeff and Nancy Hagstrom bought Newton Business Machines (Brattleboro, Vermont) to fulfill their dream of owning a business, and to avoid a commute over 100 miles per day after the business Jeff worked for moved. Their business plan was a factor in securing the necessary financing, according to Lou Dunham, Senior Vice President at Vermont National Bank. "The Hagstroms and Newton Business Machines are a good marriage," Mr. Dunham says. "Not only are they delightful people whose level of enthusiasm is exciting, but they also came to me with a thorough, well-thought-out business plan which allows us to structure a loan to meet the business's needs."

Part of that plan was a line of credit to handle accounts receivable. A cash flow projection (monthly for the first year, quarterly for the next two) highlights periods when additional capital might be needed. Although sufficient equity investment is also necessary, it isn't enough to ensure ongoing success for the business.

"Even though sales have been up every month," Mr. Hagstrom says, there's still that lag of at least 30 days until most sales turn to cash. For a business like ours, the availability of adequate working capital is the lifeblood that keeps us going."

Having prepared a detailed business plan you are now in a position to spend the necessary time to understand the true financial requirements of your business. A little time and effort now will return great dividends in the future. There are numerous textbooks on financial management and plenty of courses and seminars to take. Check with SCORE and SBDC counselors; they are used to helping people learn financial management techniques. Your banker and accountant can also help. You don't have to become a financial wizard. You will have to understand the principal financial statements (balance sheet, profit & loss, cash flow) and concepts such as break-even analysis and ratio analysis. These are basic business management accounting tools, and their use should become second nature to you.

Inadequate capitalization has been cited by Dun & Bradstreet as the number one reason for business failures. It is one thing to buy a residence that strains your resources; it is quite another to buy a business that leaves you with no margin for error.

Proper capitalization involves an analysis of two areas: 1) the capitalization necessary to purchase the business and fund its first year of operation, and 2) the capitalization necessary to implement the growth identified in your five-year plan. In the purchase of your business it is necessary to consider the down payment; adequate working capital; and a reasonable contingency or emergency fund that will permit you to withstand unexpected reverses. These requirements should be clearly detailed in your business plan; they also are important pieces of the Business Evaluation Form (see page 74).

The balance sheet and cash flow projections in your business plan are keys to the proper amount of capital needed both to buy the business and to fund its operation for the first three years. It is important in your discussion with a banker not only to outline your cash needs to purchase the business but also the needs over the first three years. The balance sheet provides information which, expressed in ratios, enables comparison to industry norms. The cash flow will not only indicate the amount and timing of possible credit needs, but as a bonus becomes the backbone of your financial controls when used as a **cash flow budget.**

Your banker will want to closely examine both the balance sheet and the cash flow to help determine what kind of credit makes sense for your business; this is where your business plan is used most effectively as a financial proposal. Your assumptions, experience, and credibility factor in as well. Don't be surprised if you have to sign personal guarantees for your small business' debts. As one banker put it, "All loans to small businesses are personal loans."

Part of the difficulty in determining the proper amount of capitalization is an inherent ambiguity in the term "capital." As used in this section, capital represents the permanent investment in the business by the owner plus retained earnings. Capital in this sense includes subordinated debt (cash you lend the business on a quasi-permanent basis). You can't pay down subordinated debt without your bank's permission, so they consider it to be capital. Your accountant can explain the tax advantages of subordinated debt over contributed capital, but whether your investment is all cash or a combination of cash plus debt, your money will be at risk.

Another use of the term appears in "working capital." Working capital is calculated by analyzing the funds needed to finance the growth in inventories, accounts receivable and operating expenses or may be calculated by subtracting liabilities from current assets. You need adequate working capital—"adequate" meaning "within acceptable trade ratios," which will be discussed below—to meet short-term obligations.

Net worth (book value, composed primarily of contributed capital plus retained earnings) is defined as total assets minus total liabilities. The effects of inadequate capital ripple through the balance sheet, showing up as low or negative retained earnings, excessive debt (both long and short-term), and—most dangerous for a small business— as a weak working capital position. Bankers and other investors (including trade suppliers) view inadequate working capital with justifiable alarm.

To make things even worse, too little capital leads to excessive borrowing which leads to higher interest costs, lower profits, tight cash flow, and weak competitive position. So while capital is a balance sheet item, it affects the profit and loss as well as the cash flow. Once you understand this, the problem of capitalization will assume its proper importance.

Finally, don't be worried about having too much capital. No business ever went under because it was overcapitalized.

How do you estimate and secure adequate capitalization for your business? Three factors help you determine the proper level of capital for your business:

1. **Facts.** There is no substitute for research. Ignorance, optimism, wishful thinking and greed are among the strong factors that lead to undercapitalization. Facts are a great antidote to these dangers. If you have a limited amount of capital, plan accordingly, because additional capital is not always available at a price you'll be willing to pay. It is necessary to limit growth to the level consistent with your ability to fund it.

2. **Carefully prepared cash flow balance sheet, and profit and loss projections.** You need these to calculate the amount of capital your business needs now and in the foreseeable future. This is particularly important if your plans involve growth or radical change in the way the business conducts its affairs. Business history is strewn with the failures of small companies who experienced a rapid rise in sales and profits but who failed because they did not properly plan for the capital necessary to finance the growth in inventory, accounts receivable and operating expenses. Depending on the amount and size of growth you may not be able to assume that the banks will provide the increased funding. Additional equity investors may be required. These projections are an integral part of your business plan, and were prepared in Step Four.

3. **Trade financial figures.** Use of the information contained in Robert Morris Associates' *Annual Statement Studies* or Prentice-Hall's *Almanac of Business and Industrial Financial Ratios* is invaluable in making sure that your estimates are well-grounded. Your banker and other potential investors use these to help evaluate and understand your financial projections. Trade associations and publications are another excellent source of industry specific ratios and allow you to compare your plans against the norms, forcing you to analyze and understand any difficulties that may exist.

This section also mentions a number of possible sources of financing. A rule to follow is to obtain funds wherever the interest rate and pay-back terms are most favorable. If you have borrowable cash value in life insurance, for example, use it to the fullest, as the interest rate is far lower than on commercial loans. If you plan to keep your present residence and it is not fully loaned up, you can probably borrow on it at a lower interest rate than the prevailing commercial rate.

The following pages are designed to help you determine what adequate capitalization for your business means.

Determining the Working Capital Requirement

Step Three: Proper Acquisition Price and Terms, and Step Four: A Reasonable and Complete Business Plan, provide the information you need to determine what adequate capital for your business will be.

From the Business Evaluation Form (Pages 74 to 80): Determine the total investment including the inventory and working capital requirements considering:

Line 30: Inventory and Working Capital Requirements
Line 50: Total Investment
Line 51: Down Payment
Line 52: Balance to be Financed

Line 30 of the valuation should be compared to the balance sheet to determine any adjustments that are necessary. Calculating working capital requirements is a complicated procedure, and you may want professional assistance the first few times you try to figure it. In a simple form it requires an analysis of:

Average Inventory   _____
Plus Accounts Receivable   +   _____
Subtotal   _____
Minus Accounts Payable   -   _____
Subtotal   _____
Plus any additional Working Capital   _____
Needs (i.e., salaries, operating supplies)   _____
Total Working Capital

In an ideal situation you would get paid for all your goods or services *before* you had to pay your vendors or employees. This is usually not the case and the difference is the working capital you need. The working capital needed to buy the business and fund its first year of operations is different from that needed to fund normal operations. You should understand both. *The Business Planning Guide* details the development of the cash flow projections. Completion of these projections will assist in developing a proper working capital analysis.

Using Financial Ratios

Properly used, an analysis of balance sheet ratios is a useful tool in the analysis of the business and the existence of adequate capitalization. When compared to industry standards or other companies, ratios help to identify strengths and weaknesses.

Ratio analysis is helpful in the valuation process when determining the multiple to apply to excess earnings ratios. If the ratios are better or worse than industry standards, that should influence your thinking.

You should develop your ratio analysis not only on the basis of historic performance, but also after aquisition: How does the balance sheet look with the new financing and debt structure in place? The new and old ratios should be compared to industry averages so that you fully understand the impact of all changes.

Following are some common ratios to be analyzed:

1. Liquidity Ratios - Indicate the ability of a company to meet its current obligations

Name	Formula	Use
1. Current Ratio	Current Assets / Current Liabilities	Indicates ability to pay short-term liabilities on time
2. Acid test (quick ratio)	Cash + Accounts Receivable + Inventory / Current Liabilities	Indicates ability to pay short-term liabilities on time

2. Activity Ratios - How efficiently a company uses its assets

1. Inventory turnover	Cost of goods sold / Average Inventory	Indicates degree of liquidity plus identifies obsolete or slow moving inventory situations
Number of days in inventory	365 / Inventory Turnover	
2. Accounts receivable turnover	Annual Sales / Average Accounts Receivable	Analyze liquidity identifies slow collection situations
Number of days sales in accounts receivable	365 / Accounts Receivable turnover	
Sales to Fixed Assets	Sales / Fixed Assets	What is the efficiency of the assets in generating sales

3. Leverage Ratios - Long-term financial strength of the company

1. Total debt to total assets	Total liabilities / Total Assets	Defines total debt of company that is provided by creditors vs total assets.

2. Debt to Equity

$$\frac{\text{Total Liabilities}}{\text{Total Equity - Intangible Assets}}$$

3. Fixed Charge Coverage

$$\frac{\text{Earnings Before Interest \& Taxes}}{\text{Interest \& Leases \& Current Portion Long-term Debt + Notes}}$$

Ability of company to cover debt and fixed obligations

4. Profit and Loss Ratios - Measure operating performance

1. Gross Profit/Sales

$$\frac{\text{Gross Profit}}{\text{Sales}}$$

Measure of Gross Profit vs Industry

2. Operating Profit/Sales

$$\frac{\text{Operating Profit}}{\text{Sales}}$$

Measure of Operating Profit vs Industry

3. Pre-tax Income/Sales

$$\frac{\text{Pre-tax income}}{\text{Sales}}$$

Measure of pre-tax income and Treatment of depreciation and interest

4. Net Profit/Sales

$$\frac{\text{Net Profit}}{\text{Sales}}$$

Comparison to industry

5. Return on Investment Ratios

1. Return on Equity

$$\frac{\text{Net Income}}{\text{Average Common Stock-holders Equity or Total Investment.}}$$

After tax or return on share-holders total investment

2. After tax return on total investment

$$\frac{\text{After Tax Equity Income}}{\text{Down Payment}}$$

Return on your invested cash

3. Return on total assets

$$\frac{\text{Net Income + Interest}}{\text{Average Total Assets}}$$

How efficiently is company using assets

Keeping the ratios within reason is a tougher stunt than first appears. This is another area where competent professional advice is useful. The aim is not to produce a clone of the trade average, but rather to make sure that you have a financially sound business, where differences from the norm have an understandable and legitimate reason, and are based on your resources and business conditions that you are facing.

Summary

The capital you need consists of three parts: the cash you need for the down payment (or outright purchase) of the business, the working capital needs for the first year of operation and the working capital needs for the first three years of operation. In calculating adequate capitalization, it is especially important to pay attention to working capital needs, and, because any major business transition involves unforeseen problems, a cushion for liquidity just in case is simply good insurance.

Since most bankers use Robert Morris Associates' *Annual Statement Studies* to justify their decisions, make sure that your ratios—especially leverage ratios such as debt to worth—are in line. While you may have substantial deviations, be prepared to proffer acceptable, rational, well-founded reasons for such deviations.

Balance Sheet Information

	Last Yr.	Current Yr.	After Acquisition	Industry Average
Current Assets:				
Cash				
Accounts Receivable				
Inventory				
Prepaid & Other				
Total Current Assets:				
Fixed Assets (NET):				
Plant & Equipment (Net)				
Other non-current assets:				
Intangibles ("Goodwill")				
Total Fixed Assets:				
Current Liabilities:				
Accounts Payable				
Current Portion Long Term				
Other Current Liabilities				
Total Current Liabilities:				
Long Term Debt:				
Total Liabilities:				
Net Worth:				
Capital & Sub. Debt				
Retained Earnings				
Total Net Worth:				
Total Liabilities & Net Worth:				
Key Ratios:				
Current Ratio				
Acid Test				
Debt/Worth				
Working Capital:				

Sources of Financing

Financing Source	Type of Financing	Purposes
Commercial Banks	Accounts receivable, inventory, floor plans for equipment, auto dealers, etc., indirect collections	Short-term commercial loans and/or lines of credit
	Equipment purchase, equipment leasing real estate, working capital	Long-term debt (term loans)
Savings Banks & Thrifts*	Real estate	Long-term debt
Commercial Finance Companies	Accounts receivable, inventory, factoring	Short-term debt (lines of credit)
	Equipment loan, equipment leasing, real estate	Long-term
Consumer Finance	Personal property loan	Short-term and/or long-term
Factor	Factoring receivables	Short-term (line of credit)
Government		
EDA	Direct-term loans loan guarantees	Long-term
Farmers Home	Term loan guarantees	Long-term
Local Development Companies	Facilities/equipment financing	Long-term
Small Business Administration**	Line of credit guaranteed, loan guarantees: lease guarantees, contract performance, term loan guarantees	Short-term

*In some states, savings institutions may be allowed to offer a limited range of commercial bank services, including commercial loans. However, your best bet for a commercial loan is a commercial bank.
**Check with your local SBA for a thorough, up-to-date breakdown of available programs. They change frequently but provide such excellent services that it will pay you to keep abreast of their programs. The SBA can also keep you informed of the availability of other government programs.

Sources of Financing (continued)

Financing Source	Type of Financing	Purposes
Leasing Companies	Equipment leasing	Long-term
Life Insurance Co.'s	Policy loans, real estate, working capital	Short/long term long-term
Venture Capital: Professional	Start-ups, growth	Equity debt (esp. convertible)
Venture Capital: Non-Professional	Start-ups, growth, working capital	Equity, debt convertible debt
Small Business Investment Co. (SBIC)	Equipment loan, equipment leasing, real estate term loans, working capital	Long-term debt
Minority Enterprise SBIC (MESBICS)	Start-ups growth working capital	Equity: Stock debentures, convertible debt

Thirty Potential Sources of Financing

1. Banks
2. Family and Friends
3. Business Acquaintances
4. Employees
5. Suppliers
6. Customers
7. Venture Capitalists
   a. Wealthy Individuals and Families
   b. Established Venture Capital Firms
   c. Bank Subsidiaries
   d. Small Business Investment Corporations
   e. Venture Capital Subsidiaries of Companies (G.E., Ford, Singer)
8. Investment Bankers/Stockbrokers
9. Factoring Institutions
10. Commercial and Consumer Loan Companies
11. Small Business Administration
12. Investment Clubs
13. Local Development Groups (City, Country)
14. State & Regional Business Development Councils
15. Pension Funds
16. Corporations
17. Leasing Companies
18. Investment Advisers and Business Agents
19. Management Consultants
20. Auditing Firms
21. Veteran's Administration
22. Real Estate Investment Trusts
23. Endowed Institutions
24. Credit Unions
25. Economic Development Agency
26. Insurance Companies
27. Mutual Funds
28. Tax-exempt Foundations
29. Charitable Trusts
30. YOU

Step Six:
Applying Fundamentals of Good Management

CASE IN POINT

Darrol Robinson, owner of Damar Plastic & Metal Fabricators (Somersworth, New Hampshire), made a tough decision: He was going to sell the metal and plastic component company he had founded in 1974, even though its sales and profits had grown steadily through the years. He had reached a point where the administrative demands a growing company places on its owner were no longer enjoyable.

"What impressed me about Damar," says Don Giancola, the CBI associate who handled the sale, "was how well-organized the business was, and the challenge was to find a buyer who would capitalize upon this foundation to take Damar through the next level of its growth."

Mr. Robinson says that "One requirement was that the next owner be a manufacturing company, rather than an individual, whose strengths would dovetail with Damar's. Another concern was for my employees. Last but not least, I wanted the new owner to have the financial wherewithal to fund Damar's growth."

Christopher Bond, president of F.W. Morse and Company (Saco, Maine) filled the bill. "Chris was a walking success story," Darrol says. "He had all the qualities we were looking for: youthfulness, enthusiasm, management and administrative skills, fortitude, positive track record, and exposure to a product-oriented business."

When Chris acquired F.W. Morse in 1985, it was losing money. Though it became profitable under his ownership, its manufacturing technology was weak. "We didn't have the capability to make parts we knew customers needed," Chris explains. "If we were to grow, we were going to have to acquire a company that had the manufacturing abilities we needed."

Damar fills a manufacturing need for F.W. Morse; F.W. Morse brings complementary administrative and marketing skills to Damar. And the balanced blend of skills Chris brings to the merged companies guarantees their success.

No one should consider small business ownership without experience or knowledge in the basics of business management. There are hundreds of education programs around the country that can provide this basic knowledge. A career in corporate management will be valuable preparation for business ownership, but will usually need to be augmented by courses in accounting or small business management. This is because success in small business demands that you be generally good at a wide range of activities, while corporate experience tends to demand expertise in a narrow range.

Most of the mistakes we have seen in looking at hundreds of small businesses were mistakes involving relatively simple matters that could have been avoided by following the rules outlined in any good basic management textbook. Careful attention to applying these basic rules will pay great rewards and give you a competitive advantage. Most small businesses are managed indifferently if at all.

There are many excellent small business management textbooks. Every business owner's personal library should include several such texts and they should be referred to constantly. The bibliography in Step Seven below contains several references.

Every business owner should plan in advance to continually strengthen his or her management skills. Effective management requires a continually steep learning curve. Commit yourself to a regular learning and review program.

Some suggestions:

- Stay current with trade magazines and literature in your field. You will find that a librarian, versed in research skills, will be a valuable (and cost-effective) ally. Local college or university libraries are particularly rich sources of information and advice.

- Join trade associations relevant to your business. The costs are trivial and the benefits great. Cultivate a working relationship with the editor of the trade magazine; he or she will be on top of trends, changes, and other factors that you should be aware of.

- The Small Business Administration's best programs are educational and supportive in nature. Inquire about the Small Business Institute (SBI) and Small Business Development Center (SBDC) programs by calling the nearest SBA office. (Look in the white pages of your phone book under "United States Government, Small Business Adm.")

- SBI's are university based programs geared to helping going concerns. SBI instructors are business faculty members with a small business bent; ask them to help you assess your own management strengths and weaknesses, or refer you to other courses of study.

- SBDC's provide excellent one-on-one management counseling, and most run seminars and workshops on highly specific management topics. SBDC counselors pride themselves on facilitating business and marketing plans, and have access to a wide range of inexpensive SBA information and other material.

- A number of SBA studies indicate that the most successful small business owners make regular use of outside professional advisors. It will pay you to have an excellent accountant and a fine "can-do" business attorney. It may also be worthwhile to locate a consultant in the field you are entering to help you set up basic systems and to provide you with a periodic "management audit." Never be too proud or independent to take such guidance. A good consultant will perform such services for a small fraction of the benefit that can be obtained by following his or her advice.

How do you find these professional advisors? Ask your banker and other small business owners for references, then follow up on the referrals. You will find that a small number of names will crop up repeatedly. A good business broker will be helpful here; he or she has to know who is capable and who is not. Choose from these, keeping in mind that you will be working closely and confidentially with them, so personal chemistry is an important factor. (And remember that if things don't pan out with any of them, you can choose another.)

The Good Management Scorecard may be of help to you. It covers twenty areas of basic good management. Consistent application to these areas tends to be the hallmark of the most successful enterprises. If you can score at least 5 in most of the areas, you are probably doing a better job of management than most of your competitors and in small business, doing better than your competition is the equivalent of success.If you score 3 or lower in any area, you should concentrate your attention on that area. Avoid the trap of spending all of your time doing the things you do best. This leads to lopsided management and certain trouble. Often, a well-managed business is one where nothing is being done badly!

The Major Pitfalls in Managing a Small Business is suggested reading as an adjunct to the Scorecard, especially if you haven't run a small business before. Small businesses, traditionally undercapitalized, just don't have the resources to survive major blunders. Fortunately, most major blunders are avoidable.

Summary

The general skills that effective small business management calls for can be learned, from both formal and informal sources. Using competent advisors makes sense: it multiplies the experience and skills available to your business, and since the correlation between small business success and use of outside advisors is so high, only a fool would be too shy or arrogant to seek such assistance. Improving your own management skills leads to the incremental improvement of your business over time, which is the surest way to solidify the gains you hope to make.

Most small business owners don't approach management with this level of professionalism. Take advantage of this. Your competitive advantages will be multiplied.

20 Rules for Success in Small Business Management: A Scorecard

Good management requires constant, objective analysis of the strengths and weaknesses of a business.

By rating yourself objectively and truthfully in each of these areas of management, you can define a program that will inevitably lead to both business and personal growth.

Use the scale on the right for your own ratings. If you score less than 5 in any area, it is a sign that you should take steps to improve performance. You can probably afford to ignore the areas where you score 9 or 10.

Growth and success are the result of regular attention to these basics. Stagnation or failure virtually always result from easily identified shortcomings in one of the categories listed below.

Management Category

1 2 3 4 5 6 7 8 9 10

I. Select a business carefully

A. Consider only a business that meets these standards:

1. Good records.

2. Full disclosure.

3. Growing market (above the inflation rate).

4. Profitable now or route to profitability can be readily identified.

5. Market not saturated.

II. Evaluate the business carefully

A. Use a proven evaluation method.

B. Get professional tax planning counsel.

C. Pay no more than business is worth

Management Category   1 2 3 4 5 6 7 8 9 10

III.   Is the business properly capitalized?

A. Base your capitalization needs on "worst-case planning."

B. Have emergency funds or access to them.

C. Structure acquisition terms to avoid unnecessary tax problems or excessive debt-service load.

IV.   Prepare a complete business plan

A. Project results at least three years ahead.

B. Include budget for required new capital expenditures.

C. Revise Plan annually.

V.   Prepare a complete marketing plan

A. Know the demographics of your market.

B. Define the market to be served.

C. Define underlying concept in terms of marketplace need. Eliminate inconsistencies in the business.

D. Analyze competition.

E. Define share of market, now and future.

F. Define marketplace positioning (Price, Quality, Service, Convenience).

G. Define the "Unique Selling Proposition" of your business. How does it differ from others?

H. Identify other products, services, markets that can be developed with timetable for development.

Management Category   1 2 3 4 5 6 7 8 9 10

VI.   Monthly budgets and statements

A. Identify fixed and variable costs.

B. Use accrual method for regular statements.

C. Include standard cost comparisons.

D. Keep records up-to-date and thorough.

F. Prepare regular cash flow projections.

VII.   Develop a company "look"

A. Pay attention to non-verbal communications
(appearance, design, cleanliness, etc.).

B. Work for consistency of appearance and design.

VIII.   Establish strong
trade/business relationships

A. Get help and information from suppliers.

B. Cultivate good banking relations.

C. Take part in industry activities.

D. Cultivate "centers of influence" in your field.

IX.   Develop an information base

A. Keep track of new developments in industry.

B. Obtain and study all key trade information.

C. Understand the "state of the art" in your
business.

D. Provide customers with best available
information relating to use of your products
or service.

E. Develop reputation as an expert in your field.

F. Require employees to be informed.

Management Category	1 2 3 4 5 6 7 8 9 10

X. Develop an innovation program

A. Budget for Research & Development.

B. Field test promising new programs.

C. Limit the risk in any new ventures to acceptable limits.

XI. Develop customer feedback

A. Use customer questionnaires when appropriate.

B. Listen carefully for indications of dissatisfaction.

C. Correct weaknesses immediately.

XII. Use outside professionals when needed

A. Budget adequately for consultants.

B. Learn to take advice.

C. Insist on objective input.

D. Take immediate action on sound recommendations.

XIII. Develop a management methodology

A. Outline each job to be done in terms of easy-to-follow steps and procedures.

B. Use checklists to prevent harmful lapses.

C. Use written job descriptions.

D. Develop written policies.

E. Conduct regular progress and evaluation meetings.

F. Insist on good performance.

G. Encourage input from staff.

Management Category   1 2 3 4 5 6 7 8 9 10

XIV. Continually improve your management skills

A. Develop regular reading/study habits.

B. Take courses every year to improve skills.

C. Make yourself dispensable by developing strong employees.

XV. Set ambitious goals

A. Use Business Plan to define goals.

B. Compare performance with top rank of competitors.

C. Be the pace-setter in your defined market.

XVI. Aim for high quality

A. Retain only employees who really care personally about the company's quality.

B. Establish high product/service standards.

C. Do not tolerate shoddy performance.

D. Design products/services for top of market.

E. Stand behind your products or services.

F. Never be satisfied with your performance.

G. Pay good employees well.

XVII. Develop a planned maintenance/replacement program

A. Prepare for unexpected replacement.

B. Maintain facilities in top condition.

C. Use company appearance as a statement of your standards to customers.

Management Category   1 2 3 4 5 6 7 8 9 10

XVIII. Develop problem-solving abilities

A. Never panic.

B. Understand how to examine options.

C. Always get facts behind a problem.

D. Always understand the "downside risk" of a decision.

E. Make decisions promptly.

F. Do not try to be 100% right.

XIX. Abandon losing programs

A. Avoid emotional commitments to programs.

B. Avoid too much ego involvement.

C. Change course when evidence is clear.

D. Plan changes in course to minimize negative effects.

E. Listen to differing opinions.

XX.   Know your competition

A. Investigate competitive companies regularly.

B. Never be defensive about competitive products or services.

C. Adopt effective programs used by competitors when practical.

D. Try to outperform competitors in all-important areas of service

The Major Pitfalls in Managing a Small Business

Problem*	Solution(s)
Lack of experience	Attend seminars, take courses in small business management, acquire and use information contained in books and pamphlets, use consultants and other professionals, talk with small business owners. Be aware of your limitations and strive to turn them into strengths. Focus on success.
Lack of money	Put together a well-thought-out business plan and get outside help with it. Be conservative in your projections of income and liberal in estimating expenses. Listen to your accountant and your banker. Strive for quality. PLAN, PLAN, and PLAN again. Buy and use the Business Planning Guide.
The wrong location	It is said that there are three critical factors in a retail business—location, location, and location. Use Bureau of Census data as well as information on traffic count from your state highway department.
Inventory management	Analyze turnover constantly. Don't over buy. Find out what customers want. Use a computer for a perpetual inventory count. Sell off slow-moving stock.
Too much capital in fixed assets	Examine the merits of leasing as opposed to buying. Subcontract items that you can't produce economically. Stick to your business plan regarding fixed asset purchases. Analyze and justify all new purchases from a profit standpoint. Watch the tendency to buy too soon.
Poor credit practices	Don't give credit unless you have to. Use bank credit cards. Screen new credit applications carefully. Limit open credit purchases. Manage and age your receivables.
Taking too much for yourself	Don't get greedy and don't use the checkbook balance as any indication of your solvency. Plan your salary like any other expense and stick to it.
Unplanned expansion	Use your business plan as a forecast. Fight the natural tendency to grow as fast as you think demand is pushing you. Get good advice on capital requirements for planned expansion.
Having the wrong attitude	The right attitude is to serve others first. By that, you will serve yourself. Secondly, you must see yourself as a success in your venture.

* Each of the nine problem areas is based on findings from "The Pitfalls in Managing a Small Business" by Dun & Bradstreet, New York, NY.

Step Seven:
Effective Use of Information Resources

CASE IN POINT

Lyman Louis, the new owner of Quickprint (Rutland, Vermont) knows the print business. He has a Bachelor of Science degree in print management from Carnegie and over twenty years experience with major New York publishers, culminating in a stint as vice president, inventory and management at Macmillan. But he hadn't bought a business before.

Don Merkle, the Country Business, Inc. associate who handled the transaction, says one advantage he had was that he knew the market for printing businesses in New England. "Not only did we have all the industry data at our fingertips, we also had readily available points of reference to help us determine the value of Quickprint, as well as the market for buyers."

Mike Flynn, Mr. Louis's accountant, began looking at the transaction from a tax planning perspective, making cash flow projections and evaluating financing alternatives. "The most important issue for the buyer to address is having adequate capital to run the business," Mr. Flynn maintains. "That's why it is so important to do the financial projections. Of course, these are expected by bankers and investors. But more important, the projections tell the buyer whether the deal makes sense. If they are done accurately, they can give even more information, such as what would be needed if the rate of interest increased two points. Fortunately, Don made sure we had all the information available."

After the purchase and sale agreement was signed, the next step was for Don to help Mr. Louis write the business plan. "This exercise has three objectives," Don says. "One is to see whether the deal makes sense. The second is for the buyer to become thoroughly familiar with the business. The third is to create a financing proposal, since we were looking for one quarter of the funding to come from a bank. Here a major benefit of a well-written business plan is that a borrower can save anywhere from one-half to two points of interest, since the bank knows the loan for a carefully thought-out business is less of a risk."

The best-kept secret about small business is the incredible wealth of information and assistance that is available to an owner. Learning how to find and use appropriate information is one of the keys to success—perhaps, in the long run, the most important key of all, since there are virtually no problems that cannot be solved and few realistic goals that cannot be met with the support of accurate, useable, timely information.

Unfortunately for the new owner, there is no single place where this information can be obtained. The search method outlined in the following pages, including the limited bibliography, will help you fashion an "information base" that you can use for successful business management.

Every owner, without exception, should attack the project of building such a base almost as a first order of business. Some books you will want to buy, some will be available at libraries, SBDC's, schools or other locations. Your aim is to have access to and use of the information they contain.

Take your reference librarian to lunch. He or she deserves at least that much for the help they will provide you. Librarians are trained as research professionals, and are a notably underutilized resource for small business owners. Your local library may not contain what you need, but it can usually (through interlibrary loans) get you the information you are seeking.

We recommend that your base contain information in each of the following categories:

1. *General business management.* At least one excellent basic text on small business management is essential. Fortunately, there has been a proliferation of such books in the past few years, so your choice is wide.

2. *Business operations literature.* Excellent brochures or books are available that outline basic business operations in most fields. An example is the *Restaurant and Food Service* manual from the Bank of America's Small *Business Reporter Series.* Many of these manuals are invaluable and will give you a competitive advantage that otherwise would take you years of experience to develop. The *Small Business Sourcebook* is another quick source of where-to-find operating manuals that are specific to your business.

3. *Market Information.* Up-to-date, accurate references on marketing and market planning are essential. *Characteristics of the Population* for the market area served is an example of an essential tool in analyzing, profiling, and segmenting the market.

4. *Industry Information.* Every owner should subscribe to one or more trade publications in the field. Most trade publications publish annual supplements that are of special value in that they aid in pinpointing trends, problems, techniques, traps and other such current information that are industry-specific. Trade associations are another source of valuable information.

5. *Reference Data.* Are any reference volumes of value to you? For example, most states publish current directories of manufacturers. Many libraries contain *Thomas' Registers*, used by manufacturers or persons selling to manufacturers.

6. *Product or Service Literature.* Needless to say, a complete library of appropriate literature on products sold or services provided is essential. How-to-do-it literature of all types will help the owner and customers to get the most out of the products or services sold.

7. *Planning and Related Manuals.* There are various manuals, such as the one you are reading, on the market which are designed to make complex jobs understandable and manageable.

8. *Periodicals*. The advent of computerized periodical databases has made it possible to find articles of interest culled from literally hundreds of periodicals almost instantaneously. As an example, you can search for articles that have appeared on your industry in the *Wall Street Journal* any time in the past twenty years, and get either abstracts or copies of those articles in minutes. This has revolutionized research techniques.

9. *Videotapes and Cassettes*. You aren't restricted to books and periodicals. You may prefer to gain information via videotapes. There are several series of small business management videos available, such as *Inc Magazine*'s well-publicized series, or educational television's "Growing a Business" series. Cassettes are useful if you spend a lot of time in the car.

10. *Seminars*. General management as well as specific skill-oriented seminars are excellent sources of information. Commercial seminars (such as the Key Productivity Seminars) are usually up to date, with informed instructors who come in contact with hundreds of small businesses each year. Local seminars sponsored by chambers of commerce or similar groups are a good place to meet people and exchange ideas, indeed, the greatest value of many seminars and trade shows are the people you can meet and ideas you can exchange.

11. *Government Agencies*. Start with the Small Business Administration. Other agencies of particular importance to small business include the Department of Commerce, state development agencies, and their offshoots. Since these programs change according to which way the political and economic winds are blowing, you have to keep on top of what they have to offer. That's easy enough — most have mailing lists that you may ask to be placed on. A few phone calls a year may be enough.

12. *Schools, Colleges and Universities*. Local schools, colleges, or universities are a great source of information. Their libraries are invaluable: they usually have reference librarians who can help you find information quickly. Their faculty may offer consulting services or other forms of direct, specific, one-to-one advice in addition to more traditional classes. Extension and adult education programs are increasingly available and are often valuable.

Learn how to find the information you need. You'll find plenty of interesting (and sometimes rewarding) byways during the search. As you get more adept at ferreting out information, you will become more and more convinced that knowledge is power.

The bibliography is sketchy and admittedly biased and idiosyncratic. Use it as as a starting point; your information interests, business and management experience and familiarity with computer and other information technologies will lead you to further selections.

Some books will become constant companions. Spend a few dollars up front to buy these; they will save you time and money in the future. Others will be only sporadically necessary. Those you can borrow or use in a library.

Above all, develop a voracious appetite for information. The business race goes to the well-informed.

Step Eight:
Understanding the Marketplace

CASE IN POINT

Phillips A. Treleaven started Thorndike Press, a publishing company specializing in large-print books for the visually impaired, in the basement of his Unity, Maine, farmhouse in 1978. Before then he had been president of G.K. Hall, a large-print Boston publishing house, but had decided to go on his own and publish 15 regional books and seek out regional authors.

In 1980 he looked at the large-print market again, and decided he could produce and market better books at a lower cost than any of the large-print publishers. He incorporated Thorndike Press, sold stock to friends and former employers to raise capital, and took the plunge.

His first step was to survey the 3,500 largest public libraries. He got better than a 50% response to a lengthy survey, which strongly supported his plans to publish current best-sellers and other books of interest to older readers, who tend to have the greatest need for large-print books. Many of the survey responses included letters from librarians, saying it was high time that someone asked them what their customers were asking for rather than simply sending blown-up versions of standard health and reference works.

Partly due to this added information, Thorndike books are published on high-grade lightweight paper in 16-point print, and look like ordinary books. Competitive large-print books are oversized, and according to the survey, readers found them cumbersome.

"Marketing is the most important thing we do here," Mr. Treleaven says. The ordering and billing system are tied into a database with some 12,000 libraries listed, so Paul Garelli, Thorndike's marketing manager, can quickly find out who had bought what books, in what amounts, when, and in many cases, why.

Spurred by his understanding of what his markets wanted Thorndike to provide, Mr. Treleaven acquired exclusive large-print rights to works as diverse as Harlequin Romances and classic mystery stories, current best-sellers and more serious texts. He also streamlined the ordering process for librarians, who are usually overworked and underpaid. By understanding his marketplace, and putting his customers needs first, Mr. Treleaven built a sizeable and profitable publishing business in a competitive marketplace.

The purpose of your business is to create and retain customers. If you follow this purpose, profits follow. If you don't, you will sooner or later run out of cash.

One of the most pernicious traps small business owners fall into is falling in love with their products or services. While you should be deeply interested in your products and services in order to maintain high quality, you have to look at your offerings from your customers' points of view. How do they perceive your products? Why would they buy from you, and not from others? What can you do to make it easier, more convenient, safer for them to buy from you? What are your competitors doing to woo customers? Can you find out what your customers are looking for?

Putting your customers first is not just good business. It's the key to survival. Anything you can do to understand your markets better will pay off. The combination of insight (hunches, based on experience) and facts (gleaned from careful research and observations) will make your marketing plans effective, profitable, and exciting to implement.

If you are interested in the changes taking place in a specific industry, you can find a lot of guidance on probable future changes in industry trade publications, trade associations, or even independent research services. Most small business owners pay little attention to such information, and they never quite emerge from the survival stage as a result.

One valuable source of industry information regarding anticipated changes is the Standard & Poor's annual industry forecasts which can be found in any business library or obtained for a modest sum through Standard & Poor's offices.

The most useful guidance about responding to changes in the business environment, however, will be obtained from your ability to use *feedback*, tuning into the thousands of signs from your customers and other sources in the marketplace that can provide guidance on when to change, modify or strengthen various business activities. All of the studies on successful entrepreneurs have stressed the fact that the really successful owners have consciously sharpened their ability to tune into and use every kind of feedback. Even the monthly financial statements are a valuable feedback source. They tell you how well your resources are being used, and warn you when changes should be made.

This section contains worksheets from Upstart Publishing Company's *Market Planning Guide*. These worksheets were designed to make it easier for you to keep on top of your markets, adapting your products and services to the wants and perceived needs of your customers and prospects, and anticipating opportunities before your competitors. If you can do this, your success will be assured.

Three aspects of marketing dominate small business life: product, customers/prospects, and competition. The first set of forms centers on what you are selling, the second set on whom you sell it to, and the third set on your competition. The worksheets reflect these preoccupations, and are recommended as a starting point for your competitive and strategic market planning.

The Product Comparison Form, The Product/Service Application Worksheet, and The Product/Service Benefits & Markets Worksheet

These forms focus your attention on what you are actually selling in your business. In small business marketing, you want to match benefits with market segments. One of the best ways to do this is to look at what others are doing and learn from them. The Product Comparison Form structures this first level comparison, product by product.

Use the Product/Service Application Worksheet to examine each of your products or services in terms of features (qualities in the product independent of any customer) and benefits (the "what's in it for me" that markets seek). Keep a constant eye open for new applications; they can make a huge competitive difference, rekindle life in old products, and lead to expanded markets at low risk.

The Product/Service Benefits & Markets Worksheet is a summary form: you want to match products and benefits offered to manageable markets. The idea behind target marketing (and market segmentation) is that you can't afford to waste your promotional dollars, so you want to target those persons or businesses most likely to buy from you. These will be limited by, for example, geographical proximity, price and quality preferences, education, and a thousand other possible criteria.

Market Segmentation Worksheet, Sample Survey Questions, and Customer/Prospect Summary Form

Understanding your customers—who they are, what, why and how they buy—is the second leg of the marketing stool. Market research is probably the least well performed management task in small business. This may be because few people who aren't trained in marketing even know what kinds of questions to ask, let alone how to get the answers.

In the Market Segmentation Worksheet, the key is describing the ideal customer in as much detail as you wish. Experience will help you flesh out the description, including buying patterns. You need to do this to find more people like them.

The Sample Survey Questions are intended to stimulate your thinking. You will find particularly cost-effective help in developing surveys by consulting the nearest Small Business Institute program (one of the SBA's better college-based programs) and asking for help. If this is not available, ask local marketing professors for help. Carefully prepared and evaluated surveys are highly valuable, and professors are good at writing them. Surveys can pinpoint clusters of prospects you might not have identified, help make a better fit between what you offer and what the buying public wants, and help you use your marketing dollars more wisely than your competitors.

Keeping all of this information in order can be a chore. Use and update the Customer/Prospect Summary Form constantly; the most valuable single key to small business prosperity is keeping a steady stream of customers, past, present, and future, foremost in your thinking as you examine product, service, marketing and promotional strategies.

Competitor Information, Quick Comparison—Benefits Offered to Our Customers, and Shopping the Competition

The third leg of the marketing stool is understanding the competition. Your promotional strategies and sales success are heavily influenced by your ability to favorably differentiate your business (products, services, location, promotion and other aspects) from your competition.

The best and only way to do this is to know who your competitors are and then keep tabs on them. If you want to excel in this highly competitive arena, keep competitor files, simple manila folders, one for each major competitor. Put clippings of advertisements, newspaper articles, copies of notes or ideas or transcripts of radio and TV advertisements, any information germane to your competitor's business. Product literature, for example, can be picked up at trade shows: some marketing graybeards say gaining competitive intelligence is the only reason to go to these.

The Competitor Information and Shopping the Competition forms are useful in assembling the competitor files. Remember: the more you know about your competition, the better placed you will be to take advantage of their weaknesses and, not incidentally, to copy their strengths if and as appropriate.

The Quick Comparison—Benefits Offered to Our Customers form is another structuring device. As you gain familiarity with your newly acquired business and its competition, you will probably want to add to this form; the idea is that it affords a fast way for anyone—you, your salespeople, your customers, or your suppliers—to make a quick judgment of how you are doing relative to the competition. Fill these out often. Customers are fickle; performance stales; competitors aren't stupid.

Summary

In the long run, your business will succeed or not on how effectively you market your goods and services. Marketing affects everything you do in your business; the products and services you offer, the sales you generate, the profits you make. Financially, the only sure and long-term source of cash is operating profit, and operating profits depend on meeting the demands of your customers.

Put your customer first. Know your customers better than your competition does—and know your competition. There is no surer way to build a successful business.

Product Comparison Form

Fill these out for each product or service you offer. For the sake of simplicity, compare yours only to the leading competitive products or services.

Product/Service: _____

	Yours	The Competition's
Target markets:		
Benefits offered:		
1.		
2.		
3.		
Quality		
Price		
Improved versions		
Location		
Delivery		
Follow-up service		
Availability		
Convenience		
Reliability		
Service		
Guarantees		
Other (specify):		
1.		
2.		
3.		

Product/Service Application Worksheet

Product/Service: _____
_____
_____
_____
_____

What are its features? _____
_____
_____
_____
_____

What benefits does it produce? _____
_____
_____
_____
_____

How is it used? _____
_____
_____
_____
_____

How is it purchased (unit, bulk, with other products? Which other products?)_____
_____
_____
_____

What are other possible applications of this product/service? _____
_____
_____
_____

Product/Service Benefits and Markets

Your Product/Service	Benefits It Offers (Wants/Needs Fulfilled)	Possible Target Markets
1. _____	_____	_____
_____	_____	_____
2. _____	_____	_____
_____	_____	_____
3. _____	_____	_____
_____	_____	_____
4. _____	_____	_____
_____	_____	_____
5. _____	_____	_____
_____	_____	_____
6. _____	_____	_____
_____	_____	_____
7. _____	_____	_____
_____	_____	_____
8. _____	_____	_____
_____	_____	_____
9. _____	_____	_____
_____	_____	_____
10. _____	_____	_____
_____	_____	_____

Market Segmentation Worksheet

Fill out one of these forms for each of your products/services.

By: _____ Date: _____

Product/service: _____
_____
_____
_____

Describe "ideal customer" according to the criteria (see page 30 in the text).
_____
_____
_____
_____
_____

Describe their purchase patterns. _____
_____
_____
_____
_____
_____

What makes them "ideal customers" for this product/service? _____
_____
_____
_____
_____
_____

Sample Survey Questions

Questions on your customer/prospect survey should elicit information about who your customers/prospects are, their buying habits, their opinion of your product/service and their favored media. Be sure to make the survey easy to fill out—ask simple questions and provide limited choices for answers. For a more complete survey, get professional help from your ad agency, small business institute and local colleges.

1. Please tell us about yourself.

   Age: 20-30 _____ 30-40 _____ 40-50 _____ 50-60 _____ 60-70 _____

   Gender: M _____ F _____

   Marital status: Single _____ Married _____ Divorced _____ Separated _____ Widowed _____

   Do you have children? Yes _____ No _____

   Do you own your home? Yes _____ No _____

   Income level: Under $20,000 _____ $20,000 to $40,000 _____

   $40,000 to $60,000 _____ over $60,000 _____

   Occupation _____

   Name/Address (optional) _____

2. Do you currently buy our product/use our service? Yes _____ No _____

   If so, why do you buy from us? _____

   If not, why do you buy from someone else? _____

   Where do you buy (this product/service)? _____

   How often do you buy (this product/service)? _____

3. Could you tell us what you think about our product/service?

   Quality: Excellent _____ Good _____ Fair _____ Poor _____

   How do we compare with (our competitor's product/service)? _____

   How could we improve our (product/service)? _____

4. Where did you see or hear our ad? _____

5. What newspapers and magazines do you read? _____

   What are your favorite TV and radio stations? _____

Customer/Prospect Summary Form

By: _____ Date _____

Reviewed by: _____ Date _____

These are our most valuable customers and prospects, ranked from the top:
(Make sure you list the market segments and their criteria.)

Name of Customer	Market Segment	Criteria (See page 30)
1.		
2.		
3.		
4.		

We should target these prospects:

Name of Prospect	Market Segment	Criteria (See page 30)
1.		
2.		
3.		
4.		

We should consider these market niches:

1. _____

2. _____

3. _____

4. _____

Our customer/prospect objectives for the next year are:

1. _____

2. _____

3. _____

4. _____

Competitor Information

Prepared by: _____ Date: _____

Competitor: _____

Product/service: _____

Location(s): _____

Specific information: _____

    Years in business: _____

    Number of employees: _____

    Dollar sales: _____

    Unit sales: _____

    Market share: _____

    Financial strength: _____

    Profitability: _____

Players (include their age, experience in this business, training or education, strengths and weaknesses, and other pertinent information):

    President/owner: _____

    Outside advisors: _____

    Key employees: _____

The competition's marketing strategy:

    Pricing: _____

    Sales methods: _____

    Advertising themes: _____

    Promotion/public relations efforts:_____

Significant changes (new people, products, etc.): _____

How this competitor competes with you: _____

Comments: _____

_____

_____

Quick Comparison—Benefits Offered to Our Customers

Competitor offers	We offer
Customer seeks:	
Quality	
Exclusivity	
Lower prices	
Product line	
Product service	
Reliability	
Delivery	
Location	
Information	
Availability	
Credit cards	
Credit line	
Warranty	
Customer advice	
Accessories	
Knowledgeability	
Polite help	

Shopping the Competition

By: _____ Date _____

Competitor: _____

Location: _____

Rate 1 (poor) to 5 (excellent)   **Rating**   **Comments**

1. Appearance and design of store

2. Employees' characteristics:

   A. Telephone manners

   B. Courtesy

   C. Helpfulness

   D. Appearance

   E. Product knowledge

   F. Ability to handle complaints

   G. Ability to cross-sell

3. Availability of products

4. Convenience of location

5. Added services (delivery, etc.)

Bibliography

There is an appalling amount of junk published by even respectable publishing houses. Use your discretion. It is a wise idea to supplement this brief bibliography with suggestions from friends, other business owners, business professors, consultants, bankers and of course your librarian. You will find much valuable information if you look for it, but you don't want to waste time on useless or misleading "get rich quick without effort or risk using other people's money" publications.

The following books are among those we can comfortably recommend. They work. Look in them for references to further books and articles. Feel free to call the publishers (or if possible the authors themselves) for further recommendations.

Keep in mind that this is only a brief introductory bibliography. Good luck.

Introductory Books:

Todd, Alden. *Finding Facts Fast*. 1972 and 1979. Ten Speed Press, P.O. Box 7123, Berkeley, CA 94707. A very helpful introduction to research techniques ranging from book and directory research to interviews. Highly recommended. Saves you time and effort.

Daniels, Lorna M. *Business Information Sources*. Rev. ed., 1985. Berkeley/Los Angeles: Univ. of California Press. Excellent "how to research" source, especially the first three chapters.

Dorgan, Charity Anne, Ed. *Small Business Sourcebook*. 3rd edition, 1989. 3 vols. Gale Research Inc., Book Tower, Detroit MI 48226. This 3-volume information power-house is a must. If your library doesn't have this book, travel to one that does: it contains detailed information on where to find information for over 200 different kinds of small businesses. Among the many subjects Vol. 1 covers (for each line of business) are: start-up information, primary trade associations, educational programs and directories, reference works, suppliers to the trade, statistical sources, trade periodicals, trade shows, consultants to the industry, computer resources, and much, much more. Vol. 2 contains a comprehensive listing of government (federal and state) programs geared to small business, trade and professional organizations, and where to find written and other sources of general small business help. Vol. 3 is a supplement, with 20 more small business profiles, 23 "short profiles" and an index. The *Sourcebook* is as close to a one-stop information bank as you can find. If you only use one information source, this is it.

Useful Directories

Don't forget local sources such as the Yellow Pages, city and state directories, and local membership groups.

Guide to American Directories. Latest ed. Klein Publishing. P.O. Box 8503, Coral Springs, FL 33065. A library standard. Full of interesting sources of further information.

Encyclopedia of Associations. Latest ed. Detroit: Gale Research Inc. Lists all the associations you can imagine, and then a lot more. Every business owner will find several associations pertinent to his or her business. This is a valuable source.

State Bluebooks and Reference Publications. Latest ed. Council of State Governments, Box 1190, Lexington, KY 40578. Good directory of state information.

Sources of State Information. Latest ed. Chamber of Commerce of the U.S., 1615 H Street NW, Washington, DC 20006.

Directory of Business and Financial Services. Grant & Cote, Latest ed. Special Library Association, 235 Park Avenue South, New York, NY 10003.

On Cassette: A Comprehensive Bibliography of Spoken Word Cassettes. R.R. Bowker, New York, NY. Business audio tapes; updated annually.

The Video Source Book, David J. Weiner, Ed. Detroit: Gale Research Inc., Videotapes, including business and training categories updated annually.

Business Management

Baumback, Clifford M. *How to Organize and Operate a Small Business*. 8th ed., 1988. Englewood Cliffs, NJ: Prentice-Hall, Inc. The classic small business management textbook. It is the standard for undergraduate small business management courses, updated since its initial 1940 edition. Excellent reference work with more information than the average business owner would ever use. Superb bibliography.

Broom, Longenecker & Moore. *Small Business Management*, 7th ed., 1987. Cincinnati, OH: South-Western Publishing Company. Another classic, well-proven and useful.

Stegall, et al. *Managing the Small Business*. 3rd ed., 1982. Homewood, IL: Richard D. Irwin. This is an academic textbook and, as such, gets a little theoretical.

Timmons, et al. *New Venture Creation*. 2nd ed., 1986. Homewood, IL: Richard D. Irwin. A fascinating journey for a would-be entrepreneur. There is probably no other book on the market that does as thorough a job in preparing people for business ownership. Useful theory abounds, but it can be heavy-going for the unsophisticated.

Johnson, J.P.K. *Success in a Small Business is a Laughing Matter.* 2nd ed., 1982. Wake Forest, NC: Meridional Publications. It has been said that a mature sense of humor is a trait of successful owners and this book helps. The major drawback is that there is little substance to the material, but it is certainly entertaining.

The Pitfalls in Managing a Small Business. New York: Dun & Bradstreet. For the money that D&B charges for this brief pamphlet, it is well worth the price. They cover the eight most common mistakes that small business operators make.

The Business Failure Record. New York: Dun & Bradstreet. This short brochure is published annually by D&B and analyzes recorded business failures for a year by reason for failure, size of liability, state, and type of business. Good guide for overall indications of potential failure.

Minding Your Own Business. Federal Business Development Bank of Canada. The FBDB is Canada's answer to our SBA. Although some readers find the going too simple, this series provides the very basics for someone new to small business ownership. Write to the FBDB, Box 6021, Montreal, Quebec H3C 3C3 for current price and ordering information. They also have some industry-specific publications which are useful; ask for their list.

Small Business Reporter. Bank of America, Department 3120, P.O. Box 37000, San Francisco, CA 94137. This excellent series, available for $5 per pamphlet, covers both general small business management topics (such as "Avoiding Management Pitfalls," "Steps to Starting a Business," "How to Buy or Sell a Business") and industry-specific topics such as "Apparel Stores," "Auto Supply Stores," and so on. Very highly recommended for specific, down-to-earth advice.

Computers in Small Business
Boston Computer Society. Rather than refer to rapidly outdated books, or cluttered magazines, call the BCS at (617) 367-8080 and ask for a copy of their membership brochure. The special interest groups most helpful to you will be the "Consultants & Entrepreneurs" and "Business" groups. The membership fee of $48 per year represents the best bargain in the world of small computers: membership in two special interest groups, relevant publications, "hot lines," and generally fascinating information about how to use computers to make your life easier.

Accounting, Finance, Raising Capital
Kamoroff, B. *Small Time Operator* Rev. ed., 1989. Bell Springs Publishers, Laytonville, CA 95454. STO is a wonderful helpmate for individuals in uncomplicated retail or service businesses. There are forms in the back for basic bookkeeping records. The author is a CPA but does not draw on the accountant's tendency to cloud issues.

Walker and Petty. *Financial Management of the Small Firm*. 2nd ed., 1986. Englewood Cliffs, NJ: Prentice-Hall. Clear, sensible textbook on financial management.

Weston and Brigham. *Essentials of Managerial Finance*. 9th ed., 1989. New York: Dryden Press (division of Holt, Rinehart & Winston). A standard textbook used for undergraduate courses, this can be a little heavy-going at times but is particularly suited to small manufacturing firms.

How to Read a Financial Report. Originally published in 1973. Free from any Merrill, Lynch office. Superb. The best pamphlet of its kind ever done. Anyone who reads through it carefully will gain a reasonably complete understanding of the income statement and balance sheet (and, Merrill, Lynch hopes, never be scared by a prospectus or 10-K again). Belongs on your bookshelf.

Understanding Financial Statements, financing Small Business, Cash Flow/Cash Management. These three selections from the Bank of America's *Small Business Reporter* series are, as expected, excellent. $5 apiece. See above for ordering information.

How to Build Profits by Controlling Costs. New York: Dun & Bradstreet. A good and short treatise that should be read at least once a year by business owners.

Statistical References

fisCAL Business Analysis System. 1989 The Halcyon Group, Inc., 449 Fleming Road, Charleston, SC 29412-9904. Call 803-795-7336 for price and delivery information. "fisCAL" is far and away the best computerized spreadsheet analyzer available. If you are working with other small businesses, this is a must even if it runs on IBM or IBM-compatible computers. Comes with either or both the RMA or FRA databases (see immediately below) for fast, simple comparison to industry standards. Will analyze your financials and provide helpful, direct suggestions on how and where to improve your operations, also provides trend analysis. Better than an MBA in Finance on your staff. "fisCAL" beats the more heavily publicized programs hollow.

Annual Statement Studies. Robert Morris Associates (RMA), 1616 Philadelphia National Bank Building, Philadelphia, PA 19107. The banker's bible. Compilations of income statement, balance sheet and financial ratio information from a wide selection of industries: manufacturing, service, retail, wholesale, construction. It is the substantive reference work in accounting. Your banker will have a copy; ask for trade data on your business.

Financial Studies of the Small Business. 10th ed., 1989; published annually. Financial Research Associates (FRA), 510 Avenue J, SE, P.O. Box 7708, Winter Haven, FL 33883-7708. Key balance sheet and income statement (P&L) information; ratios; five-year trends. Arranged by asset size, sales volume, 25% most profitable. Powerful source most useful to small businesses.

Almanac of Business and Industrial Financial Ratios.. Latest ed. Englewood Cliffs, NJ. Prentice-Hall. Easier to read than the RMA, but less thorough. Found in most libraries.

Taxes

The Internal Revenue Service (look in your phone book for nearest office) has a number of excellent free pamphlets on business and tax matters, and also puts on bi-weekly seminars for new business owners which help with tedious but necessary matters such as getting the proper tax identification number, what forms to file when and so on. If you are going to do everything yourself (we recommend that you get and use a CPA, but recognize that some people like to figure their own tax load), make sure to attend one of these free seminars.

Master Tax Guide. Commerce Clearing House. Excerpts from Internal Revenue Code for businesses; excellent overall reference source for those fascinated with taxes.

Small Business Tax Control. Monthly, $89/year. Capitol Publications, Inc., 1101 King Street, Suite 444, Alexandria, VA 22314. This reference is a loose-leaf notebook for which periodic inserts are sent by the publisher to subscribers. Should only be used by tax accountants or those owners who foolishly wallow in tax matters instead of tending to their business.

Buying & Selling

How to Buy or Sell a Business. Small Business Reporter series. Bank of America. This monograph covers the very basic information about ownership conversion and is not intended to be an exhaustive reference on the subject.

Marren, Joseph H. *Mergers & Acquisitions: Will You Overpay?* 1985. Homewood, IL: Dow Jones-Irwin. Describes a plan for analyzing acquisitions. Particularly strong on pricing and negotiations.

Business Planning

Bangs, David H., Jr. *Business Planning Guide,* Rev. ed., 1989. Upstart Publishing Company, 12 Portland Street, Dover NH 03820. This is the definitive work in the field and is an absolute must for every potential entrepreneur and every current business owner. Although a little light on the marketing side, there is nothing else that comes close to the guide to help people prepare a business plan. (See *Market Planning Guide* below.)

Marketing

Bangs, David H., Jr. *Market Planning Guide,* 2nd ed.,1989. Dover, NH: Upstart Publishing Company. A manual to help small business owners put together goal-oriented, resource-based marketing plans. Includes worksheets and checklists for effective implementation of the plan. Supplements the *Business Planning Guide*. Strongly recommended.

Hayes and Elmore. *Marketing for the Growing Business*. 1985. New York: John Wiley & Sons. Excellent introduction to marketing, especially for new small business owners. Works well with Bang's *Market Planning Guide*.

"Marketing New Product Ideas." *Small Business Reporter* series. Bank of America. Good reading for those business owners who keep a constant eye open to growth through new product and service development. Well worth the $5 price.

Survey of Buying Power. Published annually. Sales & Marketing Management, 630 Third Avenue, New York, NY 10017. This excellent reference is produced every July by *Sales and Marketing Management* magazine, and gives summary demographic data on the population (numbers, buying incomes) for major cities and all U.S. counties. A must for serious retailers, this document works well with published Census Bureau data.

Predicasts Forecasts. Quarterly publication. Predicasts, 11001 Cedar Avenue, Cleveland, OH 44106. The cost of this service is beyond the reach of most small businesses, but large libraries—cities and universities—usually subscribe. The book is a compilation of all published information about any future forecasts that have been made about U.S. businesses or product/service lines. Items are catalogued by S.I.C. codes.

Law
Useful books on legal and credit and collection matters can be obtained from Self-Counsel Press, 1303 N. Northgate Way, Seattle, WA 98133. Phone (206) 522-8383 for their catalogue.

Anderson & Kumpf. *Business Law*. 10th ed., 1989. Cincinnati, OH: South-Western Publishing. This is a standard business law textbook useful as both a text and as a reference work. The law of contracts and agency are especially well-covered, and there is a complete reprint of the current Uniform Commercial Code (UCC).

Roberson, Cliff. *Businessperson's Legal Advisor*. 1986. TAB Books Inc., P.O. Box 40, Blue Ridge Summit, PA 17294-0850. Covers common legal questions for small business owners, including how to obtain needed licenses, personnel management and other important topics.

Jackson, Stanley G. *How to Proceed in Business Legally*. 1983. Englewood Cliffs, NJ: Prentice-Hall. Subtitled *The Entrepreneur's Preventive Law Guide, Federal Edition*. Clear and useful.

Government
A Survey of Small Business Programs of the Federal Government . 5th ed., 1984. Available from the Superintendent of Documents, US Government Printing Office, Washington, DC 20402 for $7. The *Survey* provides updated descriptions of government programs in all branches of the federal government, and steers you to more detailed (and timely) information. You should also check with your congressional representatives;

federal programs are in flux and much of the published information is outdated before it hits the street.

Small Business Administration, 1441 L Street NW, Washington, DC 20416. Write for their list of publications, or, better yet , pay a visit to the nearest SBA office, listed in the white pages of your phone book under U.S. Government. The SBA is a superlative source of small business help, both live and written, but the quality of their programs and publications is somewhat uneven. In spite of that warning, do not pass up the SBA. You've paid for it; it works.

Periodicals

Nation's Business 1615 H Street NW, Washington, D.C. 20062. $22/year.

Inc. Inc. Magazine. 38 Commercial Wharf, Boston, MA 02110. $25/year.

In Business. JG Press, P.O. Box 323, Emmaus, PA 18049. $21/year.

Ask your librarian for help. There is a wealth of widely scattered periodical information of value to small business owners. Try to make your questions as specific as possible; your librarian will help you define your questions so you can put these information sources to your own use.

- Check in your library's reference section for the latest edition of *Ayer's Directory of Newspapers and Periodicals,* as well as other guides to periodical literature. There are literally thousands of newsletters, trade magazines, and other highly specific sources of information.

- H.W. Wilson's *Business Periodicals Index* and their *Reader's Guide to Periodical Literature* are examples of sources of articles published on business (and other) topics. The *Index* is available on-line and on CD-ROM; this is high tech at its finest.

- Many major newspapers (*New York Times, Wall Street Journal,* etc.) are available on microfiche in most libraries; these are another superb source of topical information.

- *Inc. Magazine's Databasics.* 1984. Garland Publishing, Inc., 136 Madison Avenue (Second Floor), New York, NY 10016. Listing of on-line databases of interest to the small business owner.

Index

UPSTART
THE SMALL BUSINESS PUBLISHING COMPANY

For a free catalog listing all of Upstart's publications please write to:

Upstart Publishing Company Inc.
12 Portland Street
Dover, NH 03820

or call 1-800-235-8866